Mandated Report to OSC Regarding the VA:

VA Socialization of Violence, Abuse and Homicidal Tendencies

Dr. Richard L. Matteoli

CDR, DC, USN, (Ret.), FMF

Per:

California Penal Codes

42 U.S. Code and wic.

HOMICIDAL TENDENCIES within the VA

© *2015 by Richard L. Matteoli*

No part of this book may be reproduced **for profit** *by any mechanical, photographic, or electronic process, or in any form of a phonographic record, nor may it be stored in a retrieval system, transmitted, or otherwise be copied for public or private use – other than* **for fair use, educational purposes and/or legal counsel and use; as well as, and/or evidentiary use to proper law Enforcement Agencies** *as brief quotations embodied in articles and reviews – without prior permission of the publisher.*

PRIMO EVINCO TE
First Conquer Thyself"
Nemean Press
Carmichael, CA 95608

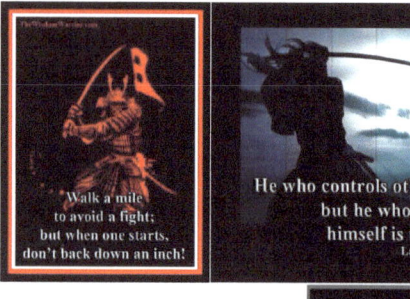

Richard L. Matteoli
Mandated Report to OSC Regarding the VA
ISBN: 978-1-943347-16-2

Acknowledgments: *John J. Whitworth*
Images courtesy Google and Facebook

From Mandated Reports, in part to the Social Body, regarding the socialization of violence and abuse. Confidentiality limits though. Per required by law: In part, Individual State Penal Codes as well as Federal Codes with wic. In Reporting Suspicions. Reports are made and sent to appropriate authorities for their decision to proceed. Being issues with and conduct therefrom the VA a Social Issue exists and the Social Body is a valid appropriate authority.

TABLE OF CONTENTS

1): MANDATED REPORT OSC Redacted Page 1

    p. 4.

2): MANDATED REPORT to OSHA on the VA

    p. 6.

3): V: VA Infantilization of Veterans

    p. 21.

4): Gaslighting: Psychological Abuse with Consequences

    p. 44.

5): Abusive Red Flagging

    p. 63.

6): IV: After Action Report to Robert McDonald and Linda Spoonster Schwartz

    p. 72.

7): III: VA GOMER Recommendations to Robert McDonald and Linda Spoonster Schwartz.

    p. 88.

8): II Report to VA re: Oakland and Phoenix

    p. 98.

9): I Report to VA re: Oakland and Phoenix

    p. 118

10): Tricare NOT Obamacare: UN-WHO Execution Codes

    p. 124

ALL CONDITIONS APPLICABLE IN ALL PRIOR MANDATED REPORTS 2005 TO PRESENT AND FUTURE

Other Evidentary Enclosures and Binders located at:
Department of Veterans Affairs
VA Revolution Board; Washington DC 20420   **INTERFERING WITH**   **TEAM**
per: OIG Civil Rights   **MANDATED REPORTER**
WHISTLEBLOWER RETALIATION: **COUNSELLING**   **PREDATION**
                                   DEFENSIVE FUNCTIONING
DoD Contractor, Contract Transferrence to VA as past Federal Employee; now retired.   **(ORGANIZED)**
5 U.S.C 2302, and Section 7 IG ACT; 41 U.S.C. 4705; 3.9 FAR, 48 C.F.R. Part 3; inclusive WPA;
UNITED STATES v. ADMINISTRATIVE: ; File Number: ; Richard L. Matteoli
Case Number: CR   MEDICAL: ; **RICHARD L MATTEOLI**

Form obtained from DOJ, San Francisco

TO OSC   **VICTIM IMPACT STATEMENT/FINANCIAL CRIME**   Re: VA AND DoD
           Per: California Penal Codes as well as Federal Codes and wic

NAME: Dr. Richard Louis Matteoli   CA State License 22647   **MANDATED REPORTER**
              SUSPICIONS REPORTING   **THANATOS: Ms. EJF**
How have you and members of your family been affected by this crime?   **ATTEMPTED KIDNAPPING**
    All VA and AFGE Employees, Contractors and anyone receiving and/or supporting renumeration of any kind

In PART and NOT Totally Inclusive Pending Further Investigations and Court Findings
VIOLATION PUBLIC TRUST, OBSTRUCTION OF JUSTICE, CIVIL CONSPIRACY
GASLIGHTING   **CONDITIONS IN PART**   RED FLAGGING

EVIDENCE DESTRUCTION; LYING TO CONGRESS;INTERFERENCE CONGRESSIONAL/LOCAL REPS;
HOBBS ACT; RICO ACT; FERES DOCTRINE; FEDERAL TORT; OCD in MASLOW HIERARCHY;
COLLUSION DoD TUCKER ACT re COMMUNICABLE DISEASES;(including) DoD ARMY FALSE STUDIES;
HONEST SERVICES; MALICE AFORETHOUGHT; COLOR of LAW/AUTHORITY; SHERMAN ACT;
PATIENT ABANDONMENT; ENDANGERMENT; BREACH of DUTY; HATE CRIME; CLAYTON ACT;
INCOMPETENCE; NEGLIGENCE; COERCION; EXACTION; QUID PRO QUO; STIGMATIC ELIGIBILITY;
DUALITY OF RESPONSIBILITY with CONFLICT OF INTEREST; AFFECTIVE BRIBERY; ROBBERY;
EXTORTIVE EXERCISE POWER, CONTROL, AUTHORITY; HOSTILE ENVIRONMENT; LARCENY;
DELIBERATE INDIFFERENCE; DELIBERATE DIFFERENCE; DOMESTICATED VIOLENCE; MENS REA;
PUNITIVE PERSONALITY DISORDER; MENS REA IN both OMISSION and COMMISSION; MANIPULATION;
FEAR CONDITIONING: STAFF; PATIENTS; APPLICANTS; POLITICAL DONATIONS; COLLUSION MET-LIFE;
TRANSFERRENCE OF AGGRESSION; PASSIVE INITIATION onto Lower Employees; INSURANCE COLLUSION;
VIOLATION FEDERAL and STATE DISABILITIES ACTS; MALIGNANT NARCISSISM; CONDUCT DISORDER;
MALIGNANT HERO SYNDROME both CLINICAL and PROCEDURAL; CODEPENDENT PSYCHOLOGY;
DENIAL DUE PROCESS; DENIAL EQUAL PROTECTION; PSYCHOLOGY of BULLYING; MAYHEM;
PATIENT, APPLICANT, Lesser Employee, MALTREATMENT and MOLESTATION; MALUM PROHIBITUM;
DISMISSIVE COGNITION with/without COGNITIVE DISSONANCE; LA LLORONA SYNDROME to ADULTS;
REFUSAL TO DIAGNOSE; MISDIRECTION IN DIAGNOSIS; EGO-SELF *imago Dei* per EDINGER;
FRAUD: CONSTRUCTIVE, IN FACTUM, MISREPRESENTATION of VETERAN, PUBLIC, WIRE, MAIL;
GOVERNMENT AGENIES Within and Outside their own; and, ELECTED REPRESENTATIVES;
WILLFUL AND WANTON DISREGARD OF PATIENT, and Public, WELL BEING; DEFENSIVE FUNCTIONING;
INFLICTION FINANCIAL, PHYSICAL and EMOTIONAL DISTRESS: ACTUAL and CONSTRUCTIVE;
ELDER ABUSE; ASSAULT AND BATTERY WITH DEADLY WEAPON; MALFEASANCE; MENACING;
VIOLATION CONTRACT including INTENT made by UNITED STATES with SERVICE MEMBERS;
LACK of SUPERVISION including: HIRING, TRAINING, CONTROL, EDUCATION of EMPLOYEES;
PRACTICING BELOW INTERNATIONAL USUAL and CUSTOMARY STANDARDS of CARE;
QUESTIONABLE CONSTRUCTION, MAINTENANCE OF CLINIC and ADMINISTRATIVE RECORDS;
QUESTIONABLE STAFF RELATIONSHIPS; HARASSMENT and SEXUAL HARASSMENT; MALUM IN SE;
DISSOCIATION SERVICE MEMBER HUMANITY; BABELIAN IMPERATIVE; DOUBLING per LIFTON;
ATTRIBUTION per DARLEY and LATANE in DIFFUSION OF RESPONSIBILITY; MALUM PROHIBITUM;
DISHONEST GAMING per ERIC BERNE in TRANSACTIONAL ANALYSIS; REPITITION COMPULSION;
DECREASING PATIENT and VETERAN VALUE within the LEGAL TRIANGLE; SUBORNING JUSTICE;
AFFECTIVE: CYCLE of BETRAYAL, CYCLE of ABUSE, CYCLE of POWER and CONTROL; HIPPA Crimes;
RATIONALIZATION INTERNAL COMMUNICATION: TRIPARTITE NATURE and STRUCTURE EGO;
FACTITIOUS DISORDER with **SELF-DEIFICATION:** GENOCIDAL PSYCHOLOGY per LIFTON;
SOCIALIZATION AND ACCULTURATION OF MUNCHAUSEN BY PROXY, IN PART;
MUNCHAUSEN SYNDROME IN SOCIAL TRANSFERRENCE; INDIVIDUATION per HUMAN SACRIFICE;
COLLECTIVE TRANSGENERATIONAL MUNCHAUSEN; MUNCHAUSEN Through SOCIAL AGENCY;
PERSONAL AND COLLECTIVE MUNCHAUSEN SYNDROME IN COLLECTIVE TRANSMISSION;
PERSONAL AND COLLECTIVE MUNCHAUSEN FOR PROFIT including, in part, for JOB SECURITY;
COLLECTIVE PROGRESSION: CULTURE BOUND and/or CULTURE SPECIFIC SYNDROMES creating
an environment of SHARED PSYCHOTIC DISORDER (FOLIE A PLUSIEURS) with aspects of
DELUSIONAL DISORDER; **ACTIVE** THANTOS with NO INVERTED SELF-REGARD per H.A. Flynt;
LIBEL; PERSONAL AND PROFESSIONAL DEFAMATION OF CHARACTER; SLANDER; MALPRACTICE;
DENIAL RELIGIOUS FREEDOM; RELIGIOUS PERSECUTION; IMPLIED CULTURAL IMPERIALISM
Influenced Through CHILD PORNOGRAPHY and INCESTUOUS PSYCHOLOGY: C.G. Jung, L. deMause;
ALL TYPES HOMICIDE DEPENDING PER FURTHER INVESTIVGATION
ATTEMPTED ENTRAPMENT FOR FALSE ARREST AND DETENTION; MISUSE MEDICAL RECORD HIPPA

ALL CONDITIONS APPLICABLE IN ALL PRIOR MANDATED REPORTS 2005 TO PRESENT AND FUTURE
Other Evidentary Enclosures and Binders located at:
Department of Veterans Affairs   INTERFERING WITH   **TEAM**
VA Resolution Board; Washington DC 20420   MANDATED REPORTER   **PREDATION**
per: OIG Civil Rights   COUNSELLING
WHISTLEBLOWER RETALIATION: **(ORGANIZED)**
DoD Contractor, Contract Transferrence to VA as past Federal Employee; now retired.
5 U.S.C. 2302, and Section 7 IG ACT; 41 U.S.C. 4705; 3.9 FAR, 48 C.F.R. Part 3; inclusive WPA;
UNITED STATES v. ADMINISTRATIVE: 343/241/njb: File Number·   ; Richard L. Matteoli
Case Number: CR   MEDICAL.   ; RICHARD L MATTEOLI

Form obtained from DOJ, San Francisco
VICTIM IMPACT STATEMENT/FINANCIAL CRIME
Per: California Penal Codes as well as Federal Codes and wic

NAME: Dr. Richard Louis Matteoli   CA State License 22647   MANDATED REPORTER
SUSPICIONS REPORTING
How have you and members of your family been affected by this crime?
All VA and AFGE Employees, Contractors and anyone receiving and/or supporting renumeration of any kind

In PART and NOT Totally Inclusive Pending Further Investigations and Court Findings
VIOLATION PUBLIC TRUST, OBSTRUCTION OF JUSTICE, CIVIL CONSPIRACY
PERSONS IN PART
Captain James A. Lovell Federal Health Center; Pediatrics
Dr. Daniel Nash, Ukiah, CA, VA Medical Clinic; VA Hospital, San Francisco, CA; in Collusion with
UCSF Medical School, San Francisco, CA; Ira Sharlip, UCSF/ARMY Possible Gilgal but non-documented;
VAOIG, John Wooditch
BVA Oakland Region, Oakland, CA in Collusion with VA Phoenix, AZ: Ulrike Willimon, Lynn Flint,
Pritz Navara(tnasingam); Ricky (Rickie) Young; Roger Caldwell-Subordinate Personality, CA State VA;
Senior Executives Association (SEA), Glen A. Costie and all executives, employees and contractors
VA Phoenix, AZ Region in Collusion with BVA Oakland Region, Oakland, CA: Sandra Flint and post
additional temporary Director Elizabeth Joyce Freeman; VAOIG; VBA, San Diego, CA
AFGE with AFL/CIO, David Cox and all executives, employees and contractors
VA Medical, Washington, DC in Collusion with DoD BUMED; DoD MEDCOM;
VA in Collusion with IRS; Lois Lerner; Gila Corporation via Hawaii VISN 21; IRS, John Koskinen
VA Medical, Washington, DC in Collusion with UCSF San Francisco, Johns Hopkins;

VA Sierra Pacific Network (VISN 21) Honolulu, HI; Palo Alto, CA; San Francisco, CA; Fresno, CA;
Sacramento, CA; Reno, NV: Elizabeth Joyce Freeman; Sheila M. Cullen;

BVA Oakland Region, Oakland, CA in Collusion with VA Sierra Pacific Network (VISN 21) and VA
Washington, DC including Board of Appeals, Resolution Board and VAOIG; Julianna M. Boor;
Michele Kwok; Leonard Lee-Subordinate Personality; Elizabeth Joyce Freeman;

San Francisco VA Health Care System in Collusion: Bonnie S. Graham; C. Diana Nicoll; Shirley A. Pikula;
Elizabeth Joyce Freeman; Dr. Ira Sharlip, USA, DoD; Dr. Thomas Wiswell; West Point; USA, False Med. Studies;

VA Minneapolis, MN in Collusion with BVA Oakland Region, Oakland, CA; and, Elizabeth Joyce Freeman;

VAOIG; Washington, DC: Richard A. Griffin; and possibly, Elizabeth Joyce Freeman;

PAVIR: (Palo Alto Veterans Institute for Research); Elizabeth Joyce Freeman; Mark Nicolls;
Phillip L. Jelsma; Lawrence L. Leung; Roberta Oka;

VA Audiology, all persons involved; VA Pharmacology Protocol Communicable Diseases all but one;
Top Line Possibly Sequestered from Information:
VA Washington, DC: Robert McDonald; Linda Spoonster Schwartz; Eric Shinseki; Allison Hickey;
Diana Rubens: Deputy Undersecretary for Field Operations, Veterans Benefits Administration, (VBA);
Laura H. Eskenazi: Vice Chairman Board of Veterans Appeals; Bruce Giles-SubordinatePersonality;
Catherine Mitrano: Deputy Assistant Secretary for Resolution Management; Elizabeth Joyce Freeman;
Iris Cooper; Wendy McCrutchen: Undersecretary for Benefits; VBA St. Paul, MN, Kimberly Graves
Leigh A. Bradley: General Counsel U.S. Department of Veterans Affairs;
Gina S. Farrisee: Assistant Secretary Human Resources & Administration;
LaVerne H. Council: Assistant Secretary for Information and Technology;
VAOIG: Richard J. Griffin; Catherine Gromek; George Opfer; Linda Halliday; Sloan Gibson; Maureen Regan;
IRS Collusion with VA: Lois Lerner; Richard Griffin; George Opfer; Sloan Gibson; Maureen Regan; VISN 21;
 Gila Corporation for false harassment debt collection; Improper confiscation Federal IRS tax returns not due;
 Marilyn Hunter, Operations Manager, AM OPS 2 (re: 04-15-2013);
IG State Department, Harold Geisel; Patrick Kennedy;
ELSEWHERE: Possible Collusion: VA Loma Linda Radiology with Loma Linda Medical School combined with
             Professor Dr. Daniel Nash VA Loma Linda Health Care Center also Palm Desert Veterans Clinic;
             AND ALL CONNECTIONS WITH GILGAL SOCIETY MASTURBATING TO BDSM CHILD PORN
             WES MORRILL; MONTEREY, CA STATE/COUNTY VA MILITARY AFFAIRS

MANDATED REPORT to OSHA on the VA
COVER LETTER
Per California Penal Codes as well as 42 Federal Code and wic

Dr. Richard L. Matteoli
CA License 22647
CDR, DC, USN, (ret.), FMF
Monterey, CA

**REQUESTING IMMEDIATE WHISTLEBLOWER PROTECTION FROM FURTHER RETALIATION FOR MYSELF;
MONTEREY VA-DoD CLINIC including DR. NICHOLAS SASSON;
MONTEREY COUNTY OFFICE, CALIFORNIA STATE VA;
USING FBI INVESTIGATION WATSONVILLE, CA OFFICE**

Documentation provided with full case before VA Resolution Board.

This request includes Report Recommendations as part of Counselling.

Prior to present circumstances involving National Security regarding a new factor introduced in linking all prior Mandated Reports it was recently reported that the NATO is studying an issue in the Middle East to individual and social acculturation of violence, abuse and PTSD. Study being conducted by a person I have long time knowledge of. NOT specifically discussed in this Mandated Report Cover Letter. Enclosures including certain physicians' masturbation video to a male genital surgical procedure on subject sent separate.

1

CONTENTS

Introduction - 3
Veteran Contractual Rights
Societal Responsibility

Subcultural Criminology - 4
MENS REA
MALUM PROHIBITUM
MALUM IN SE
MALPRACTICE
HOBBS Act
Mail and Wire Fraud
RICO Act
FERES Doctrine
Little Tucker Act
Sherman Act
Clayton Act
Homicide – Team Predation – Civil Conspiracy

Clinical Impropriety - 8
Pharmacology
Hearing Loss and Tinnitus

Disability Ratings - 9
Shared Responsibility

Reorganization - 10
Internal Structural Integration
Department of Defense Integration
External Civil Integration

VA Employee and Contractor UCMJ Accountability - 14

INTRODUCTION

VETERAN CONTRACTURAL RIGHTS
5 U.S.C. 2302, Section 7 IG ACT; 41 U.S.C. 4705; 3.9 FAR, 48 C.F.R. Part 3; inclusive WPA

1: DoD integrating with VA. EVERY Veteran signed a DoD Contract, even if Drafted.
2: Veteran proof of his/her Contract fulfillment, and how fulfilled, is the DD214.
3: Veteran Contract with DoD transfers to VA with **all** contractual rights including medical care.
4: As Contractors Veteran Rights extend EQUALLY as if the Veteran is also a **VA employee(r)**.
5: VETERANS have the right to seek WHISTLEBLOWER PROTECTION from OSHA.

DoD Directive 1241.1
Reservist Rights a Lesson for All.
1: Injury when on any kind of Duty is to be covered. There are NO minimum Days on Duty.
2: There IS NO WAITING TIME for eligibility to receive Service Related VA Care.

INTENT of CONTRACT

Contract Intent is based on Promises Made whether explicit, by inference or Common Knowledge within the social fabric. The veteran has all reasonable rights to be treated with International Usual and Customary Standards of Care and in a timely appropriate manner.

SOCIETAL RESPONSIBILITY

The woman becomes the vehicle of nature.
The man becomes the vehicle of society, the social order, the social purpose.
The woman is life. The man is the servant of life…
Life has overtaken her. Woman is what it is all about,
the giving of birth and the giving of nourishment.
Without him she would become overwhelmed.
Joseph Campbell, *The Power of Myth*.

<u>ALL</u> Service Members understand, respect and give service to and are Servants of. YET:

When does the Servant become a <u>Slave</u>?
When does the Servant become a <u>Sacrifice</u>?

There is blatant socio-functional Sexual Discrimination against males and also, at least exclusive in one respect, female Servants of Life and its Social. A demographic study of sexual ratios to occurrences of Veteran Deaths, Denials, Improper Pharmacology and Structural Avoidances of Eligibility, Access, Delays, Treatment, and *Red Flagging* is required. Immediate social maternal Life concerns that too often become out-of-hand, mostly without individual and social responsibility, do not negate Servant rights especially when Contractual.

SUBCULTURAL CRIMINOLOGY

MENS REA

MENS REA a guilty mind; the mental state accompanying a forbidden act. For an act to constitute a criminal offense, the act usually must be illegal and accompanied by a requisite mental state. Criminal offensives are usually defined with reference to one of four recognized criminal states of mind that accompanies the actor's conduct: (1) intentionally; (2) knowingly; (3) recklessly; and, (4) grossly [criminally,] negligent. The mens rea may be GENERAL, i.e., a general intent to do the prohibited act, or SPECIFIC, which means that a special mental element is required for a particular offense such as "**assault** with intent to rape" or **larceny** which requires a specific intent to appropriate another's property. In a criminal prosecution, the state must prove beyond a reasonable doubt that the required mental state coexisted with the doing of the proscribed act. Defenses of insanity, intoxication and mistake may either nullify or mitigate the existence of a SPECIFIC MENS REA. Crimes that are **malum prohibitum** often do not require any specific mens rea. See 343 U.S. 790. These are usually crimes of strict liability.

MALUM PROHIBITUM

MALUM PROHIBITUM Lat: wrong because it is prohibited: made unlawful by statute for the public welfare, but not inherently evil and not involving moral turpitude. Refers to acts prohibited solely because of the existence of statutes. It is contradistinguished from **malum in se**. For example: driving at excessive speed, is malum prohibitum because statutes prohibit as a result of a determination that it is dangerous to the community, though it may not be inherently dangerous; whereas, reckless driving would be regarded a as malum in se.

4

MALUM IN SE

MALUM IN SE - Lat: evil in itself; "naturally evil, as adjudged by the sense of a civilized community." It refers to an "**act** or **case** involving illegality from the very nature of the transaction, upon principles of natural, moral and public law." For example, murder is "malum in se" because even without a specific criminal prohibition the community would think it to be evil and wrongful act. Compare **malum prohibitum**.

MALPRACTICE

MALPRACTICE a professional's improper or immoral conduct in the performance of duties, done either intentionally or through carelessness or ignorance. The term is commonly applied to a physician, surgeon, dentist, lawyer, or public officer to denote the negligent or unskillful performance of duties resulting from such person's professional relationship with patients or clients.

Steven H. Gifis, *Law Dictionary***, Barron's**

HOBBS ACT – 18 U.S.C. §1951

Illegal for Federal Government Employees to get BONUSES and considered BRIBERY.

The HOBBS ACT prohibits actual or attempted robbery or extortion affecting interstate or foreign commerce. Section 1951 also proscribes conspiracy to commit robbery or extortion without reference to the conspiracy statute at 18 U.S.C. § 371. Although the Hobbs Act was enacted as a statute to combat racketeering in labor-management disputes, the statute is frequently used in connection with cases involving public corruption, commercial disputes, and corruption directed at members of labor unions. Jurisdiction: US Department of Labor.

> Extortion under color of official right or extortion by a public official through misuse of his/her office is supervised by the Public Integrity Section, Criminal Division.
>
> Extortion and robbery in labor-management disputes is supervised by the Labor-Management Unit of the Organized Crime and Gang Section, Criminal Division.
>
> All other extortion and robbery offenses not involving public officials or labor-management disputes are supervised by the Organized Crime and Gang Section, Criminal Division.

The three most common statutes used against Bribery are in 18 U.S.C. §666 **(a)** certain programs receiving government funding, **(b)** honest services fraud; and, **(c)** extortion under color of official right: *The coercive element is provided by the public office itself*, Evans v. U. s. 504 U.S. 255 (1992).

Some courts have held that the HOBBS ACT can be applied to past and present public officials, as well as to ones who presently occupy a public office at the time the corrupt payment occurs. The court held in the affirmative the question *whether, within the meaning of the Hobbs Act, it is a crime for candidates for political office to conspire to affect commerce by extortion induced under color of official right during a time frame beginning before the election but not ending until the candidates have obtained public office*. Courts have upheld elected officials under color of official right where the public officials induced a third party to pay out money. **(See: Congress designates IRS to pay selected VA employees BONUSES)**.

5

MAIL FRAUD - 18 U.S.C. §1341 and WIRE FRAUD – 18 U.S.C. §1343
Scheme to Defraud, deprive Honest Services, Bribery, Failure to Disclose, Conflict Interest

Mail and Wire Fraud statutes are to combat the Common Law crime of Larceny by Trick.

Mail Fraud requires: (a) scheme to defraud, (b) use of interstate communications through the Postal Service or private carrier.

Wire Fraud is through, in part: (a) telephone calls and (b) e-mails.

Involved are, in part: (a) deprive another the right to Honest Services – 18 U.S.C. §1346 arising, in part, from: (b) Hobbs type Bribery (c) Failure to Disclose (d) Conflict of Interest.

RICO ACT – 18 U.S.C. §1962
Government Employee Racketeering -> Bonuses -> with their Union as Representatives

RICO requires a Pattern of Behavior involving two or more aspects of Racketeering. Public officials are NOT exempt, but under a *Higher Standard*.

(a) Impossible to otherwise designate a government office and its official NOT to affect or NOT act through Interstate Commerce.

(b) uses, in part, Mail Fraud, Wire Fraud, Bribery, Hobbs Act violations.

(c) Requires prosecution with Forfeiture of Assets gained, fine and prison.

SHERMAN ANTITRUST ACT - 15 U.S.C. §§1-7
Government contracts, combinations, conspiracies, commerce, customer allocations

The Sherman Act prohibits (a) contracts, combinations, or conspiracies in restraint of interstate commerce or foreign trade, and (b) monopolization, attempts to monopolize, or conspiracies to monopolize interstate commerce or foreign trade. While every violation of this Act is technically a felony, the Department reserves criminal prosecution for so called "naked" or "per se" unlawful restraints of trade among competitors, e.g., price fixing, bid rigging, and customer and territorial allocation agreements. Criminal violations of this Act carry a maximum fine of $100 million for defendant (being the government is a corporation, $1,000,000 for other persons, and a maximum prison sentence of ten years per person.

Thus if deserved benefits for any reason are withheld creating victim transfer of funds as Insurance Policies, Loss of Supplemental Disability Insurance, Sale of Transportation or any asset transfer by veteran to survive through loss of income especially necessary for life and liberty a criminal act has occurred. This means if a veteran must give up monthly income so to live, a violation has occurred due to confiscation of veteran assets and Free Use thereof.

CLAYTON ANTITRUST ACT - 15 U.S.C. §§12-27; 29 U.S.C. §§52-53
Government contracts creating non-competitive monopoly

The Clayton Act prohibits corporate and other mergers – and acquisition of assets of competing companies, where the effect of such action may be substantially to lessen competition or tend to create a monopoly. Anticompetitive tying and exclusive dealing contracts are also prohibited, as are certain interlocking directorates. Violations of this Act are prosecuted civilly.

FERES DOCTRINE – 340 U.S. 135 (1950)
Cannot sue the military

The Feres Doctrine extends the English Common Law of Sovereign Immunity even from negligence. DoD transfers to the VA what it cannot, and at times will not, medically provide. This is true except in cases of non-treatment for communicable diseases endangering the public.

LITTLE TUCKER ACT – 28 U.S.C. §1346
Can sue military if released without Communicable Disease treatment as TB and STDs

Tuberculosis *is and always has been a Public Health Care concern.* California, and presumably every State in the United States, has a *Mortality and Morbidity* monthly Newsletter for all Health Care Providers to receive by mail if they choose to subscribe. This has been available since before 1970. In the 1970's California would send Emergency Notices if a local occurrence or outbreak occurred mostly due to migrants and international visitors.

The VA requires **Temporary Disability** if contact occurred in Asia or Southwest Asia. Yet Tuberculosis is area **endemic** in places as Alaska and should also be covered due to Training Exercises. If the Tuberculosis is NOT active, and at the minimum contact is shown by a positive TB test, Prophylaxis may be indicated – especially if a lung lesion, though inactive, occurs.

If Tuberculosis is active they must be isolated. Ebola patients brought to the United States should and have been properly isolated in Tuberculosis specified isolation units.

BUMED does not provide prophylaxis in certain cases, yet required necessary Liver Monitoring due to drug toxicity. The VA provides Prophylaxis but their unspoken Policy and Procedures disallows proper Standard of Care Liver Monitoring.

Yet BUMED Tuberculosis Protocol requires Prophylaxis WITH Liver Monitoring. The VA is basically a DoD extension to fulfill Contractual Obligations of the United States. BUMED Instruction: **BUMED INSTRUCTION 6224.8**

HOMICIDE - TEAM PREDATION – CIVIL CONSPIRACY

HOMICIDE any killing of a human being by another human being; most commonly used to refer to an unlawful homicide such as murder or manslaughter. "The destruction of the life of one human being by the act, agency, procurement or culpable omission of another. The destruction of life must be complete by such act or agency; but although the injury which caused death might not, under other circumstances, have proved fatal, yet if such injury be the cause of death, without it appearing that there has been any gross neglect or improper treatment by some other than the defendant... it would be homicide."

ACCESSORY one who aids or contributes in a secondary way or assists in or contributes to crime as a subordinate.

ACCOMPLICE an individual who voluntarily engages with another in the commission or attempted commission of a crime.

AID AND ABET to actively, knowingly, intentionally, or purposefully facilitate or assist another individual in the commission or attempted commission of a crime.

Steven H. Gifis, *Law Dictionary*, Barron's

CLINICAL IMPROPRIETY

PHARMACOLOGY

Improper pharmacological use of medications is a leading cause of Health Care caused Mortality and Morbidity. **Iatrogenic Pathophysiology**. The Physicians' Desk Reference is a book containing prescription drug Material Safety Data Sheets (MSDS), given by the pharmacist with each prescription. Needed is a **Directive** to *prescribe*, *treat* and if needed *test* accordingly.

It would be wise for the VA to take the lead in Health Care by setting up in each Region a *Collegial* Pharmacy Review Help-Line that will aid physicians with patients requiring a multitude of prescriptions as well as a Hot Line for professionals asking something to be reviewed without fear of Retaliation. *Quality Control.* **Always: Safety First**.

HEARING LOSS and TINNITUS

Veterans Affairs denies approximately 50,000 Hearing Loss and Tinnitus Claims for Disability annually. **ALL** denied Disability Claims must be reviewed. The VA uses only the Hearing Aid test that tests to 4000Hz. This is a Function test, as is the military's test to 6000Hz. International Usual and Customary Standards for diagnosing Hearing Loss Pathology, at the minimum, starts Diagnostic testing at 8000Hz. *Quality Control*.

The VA will then establish trained analysists that can perform all Hearing Loss and Tinnitus Disability Claims via computer communications with Agent assigned, per Agent request. Then cut and paste into Claim Decision. *Other situations may functionally apply?*

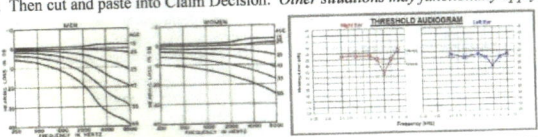

The *temporary* Tinnitus Notch for noise damage ranges from 4000Hz to 2000Hz. VA testing only to 4000Hz does not allow for a complete viewing to determine Service Connected harm which might not even necessarily be fully inclusive due to other factors as chemical contamination or pharmaceuticals.

DISABILITY RATINGS: SHARED RESPONSIBILITY

EXAMPLE: HEARING LOSS

1: Establish Legal International Usual and Customary Diagnostic Testing for Auditory Pathology to 8000Hzx
2: Maintain Hearing Aid Standards to 4000Hz
3: Use Graph similar to Example Photo.
4: Make Graph Overlay for each year of life.
5: Graph Overlay to include *Range of Normalcy*.
6: Hearing Loss Greater than Range of Normalcy is Pathology: *Unilateral - Bilateral*.
7: Establish if Service Connection applies.
8: Establish Claimant Lifestyle.
9: Establish Percent (%) Shared Responsibility if applies.
10: Shared Responsibility may be calculated as 50% Equity; or, otherwise different.

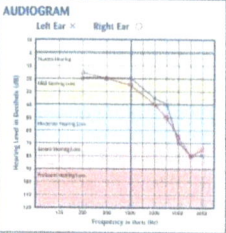

EXAMPLE: TINNITUS

1: Determine Existence and Severity of Tinnitus also with affecting **Cognitive** Hearing Loss.
2: Establish Cause and Multiple Causes of Tinnitus.
3: Establish Claimant Lifestyle and Truthfulness.
4: Establish Percent (%) Shared Responsibility if applies.
5: Shared Responsibility may be calculated as 50% Equity; or, otherwise different.

EXAMPLE: CARDIOLOGY

1: Respect civilian, other Federal and State diagnoses which are proven more correct than VA.
2: AVOID Specialist MISDIRECTION in Diagnosis using unnamed different Procedure Codes.
3: Note whether disease is Progressive or resolvable with treatment and recurrence possibility.
4: Atherosclerosis may be consolidated into this Specialty Claims Agent Responsibility.
5: Shared Responsibility may be calculated as 30%, 50% or 70% Equity; or, otherwise different.

EXAMPLE: CONSOLIDATION

1: Note that workplace Safety has increased compared to past military work environments.
2: Use all newly established Procedure Code Guidelines to be mandatory inclusion with Claim.
3: Factor *Latency* of Clinical Presentation as Heavy Metal Poisoning and **Alexithymia**-PTSD.
4: Note whether each is Progressive or resolvable with treatment and recurrence possibility.
5: Shared Responsibility may be calculated as 33% to 67% Equity; or, otherwise different.

FUTURE

1: Establish reasonable amount Specialty Case Claims Sections to interact with Claims Agents.
2: Promote to Disability Case Claims Agent from within those who have completed all rotations.
3: Promote from within to Manager Disability Case Claims Agents those who have completed a designated time as a Disability Case Claims Agent. Corpsmen, Medics extra 5% on application.

REORGANIZATION

Veterans Affairs failures are mainly structural. They are overwhelmed making inefficiency a way of life that leads to loss of discipline thus opening an avenue for criminal behavior to enter, flourish and become institutionalized.

Veterans Affairs requires *metamorphosis*, not destruction.

Metamorphosis involves a taking apart, rearrangement and putting back together. This means how it relates both as a society within itself as well as how it relates outside itself as a place within society as a whole. The following are recommendations to initiate discussion for improvement to best serve the patient that then serves society as well. This involves three basic aspects in its existence. To illustrate:

1. **Veterans Affairs Structural Integration** – Internal
2. **Military Integration** - Internal <-> External
3. **Civil Integration** - External

INTERNAL VETERANS AFFAIRS STRUCTURAL INTEGRATION

CLINICAL

1: Pharmaceuticals:

Improper use of pharmaceuticals is the leading cause of death in Health Care. It is industry wide. The VA is not different except that pharmaceutical impropriety has become its own Industrial Standard. Cure is within the grasp of Veterans Affairs. Only a couple of steps are necessary to solve this problem:

a) **Physician's Desk Reference (PDR):** Simply issue a Directive that medications, with all facets required in its dispensation and proper use are to be in accordance to the Material Safety Data Sheet (MSDS) found in the PDR and given to the patient when they pick up their prescription both *in house* and emphasis given the patient for *home care*. And, strictly enforce it.

b) **Pharmaceutical Resource Facilities:** Each Region needs to establish a *Pharmaceutical Resource Facility*. It must be *Collegial* at all times. It should be Management staffed by Pharmacists. This is where physicians can phone with questions especially regarding patients on complex medication program of treatment, a Review section that flags complex cases for review and some patients put on an update review schedule for the treating physician as well as a Hotline for VA employees with concerns and with NO FEAR OF RETALIATION. This has long time been discussed by professionals since my time stationed at Great Lakes 1984-1986. TAKE THE NECESSARY LEAD.

10

Yet, it must be noted that there is leeway in use of medications depending on the patient's condition, where they are at within the course of their Treatment Plan as well as certain times and places variation might be best to test current treatment efficacy.

2: International Usual and Customary Standards of Care: Veterans Affairs in many ways is open to liability by practicing Below the International Usual and Customary Standards of Care. One case alone, beyond improper use of medications, is the Hearing Loss and Tinnitus Pathologic examination. The VA denies approximately 50,000 such cases per year. They must all be reviewed and retesting required is **new** test is found appropriate for a correct PATHOLOGIC Diagnosis.

   a) To accomplish this correction of past impropriety each Region can set up a Hearing Loss and Tinnitus Review facility. Staffing may consist of new employees. With proper training they may become Technical Specialists for such Disability Claims. The Standard Claims Agent can forward the Test and all Clinic notes with Patient History and, if available, civilian diagnostics. The Review Specialist then does the Disability Protocol and returns the final decision to the Standard Claims Agent. If the Standard Claims Agent accepts after his/her review this then will be the official Decision to which the Clamant may respond.
   b) RESULT: creates an *Internal Review* process among Veterans Affairs professionals.
   c) This Procedural Protocol may be duplicated in other specialties and sub-specialties as Veterans Affairs deems efficient.
   d) Insurance companies hire retired and disabled physicians, dentists and other Health Care Providers on a Full Time as well as a Part Time basis.

HARD ASSET REALLOCATION: PHASE I

A main problem with Veterans Affairs is construction and maintenance of Hard Assets. The Hard Asset to be first assessed would be the VA Hospitals themselves. Hard Asset Reallocation is already part of Veterans Affairs Hospital affiliations with Medical Schools and an avenue to seriously look into this program that should be used and expanded if possible when greater efficiency is shown to be established. **Hard Asset Reallocation in use, but entirely forgotten,** is existent in at least two California Veterans Affairs agreements with two California Medical Schools. These two are:

   a) **Mather** Veterans Affairs with University of California Davis Medical School. Sacramento County sold its County Hospital to the State of California for $1 (one dollar) in which new Davis Medical School could use for both didactics yet mostly patient treatment. Yet it also maintained its County Hospital status for a treatment facility for the poor. I used to cover the Dental Clinic for a friend when gone where both the poor were treated and the Medical School patients were located for their treatment
   b) **Palo Alto** Veterans Affairs with Stanford University Medical School. Palo Alto County Hospital was merged into Stanford University Medical School in like manner as Sacramento County Hospital with UC Davis Medical School.
   c) **SOLUTION:** Sell (or Lease) all VA Hospitals to existing Medical Schools whether public or private that the VA has a relationship with. Maintenance now totally belongs to the State or Medical Schools. Phase II belongs to the VA and the DoD into the school.

DEPARTMENT OF DEFENSE INTEGRATION

Veterans Affairs is *currently integrating* with the Department of Defense.

SOFT ASSET REALLOCATION: PHASE II

At the same time Veterans Affairs sells its Hospital Hard Assets to the associated medical schools, the medical schools LEASE BACK the hospital to the VA Residencies for the same price of $1 (One Dollar) and maintain the relationship including Medical Residencies.

Soft Asset Reallocation will benefit Veterans Affairs, Medical Schools and most of all patients served as well as society in general. Put in other words, it is a win-win-win-win restructuring:

a) TRICARE is a DoD Insurance Program set up as a standard insurance company where care provided is set to Industry Standards thus allowing maneuvering to keep up with advances in Health Care, not be involved in government stagnation and not be involved in other social programs as paying a premium to fund the Death Penalty of/by its patients.
b) Medical schools may then bill Tricare, social security, private insurance
c) Monies above and beyond collection and maintenance costs may then be reallocated back to the Medical School-Veteran Affairs partnership.
d) Monies may be spent on VA requested needs as new and upgraded equipment, supplies and disposable treatment items.
e) Integration with Medical Research may be extended into non-treating colleges and Universities.
f) Electronic Shared Health Care Records, secure in each Agency, HIPPA transferred upon PROPER request and establish PROPER SOAP Noting.

PATIENT CARE REALLOCATION: PHASE III

a) Give Tricare Insurance Options to Veterans as either a Primary or Secondary Carrier.
b) Maintain focus on treating Service Connected Disabilities
c) Upgrade then maintain Increased Reserve Readiness
d) Maximize Shared Civilian Health Care Assets and Inter-service Cooperation
e) Maximize Educational Health Care Assets increasing Research Capabilities
f) Eliminates Majority Travel Reimbursements and other Ancillary Expenses
g) COST: Dental Clinics to be installed by the Medical Schools from monies provided by insurance payments.

RESTRUCTURING RESERVE HEALTH CARE ASSETS INTO VA-DoD: PHASE IV

VBA REGIONS   VHA REGIONS

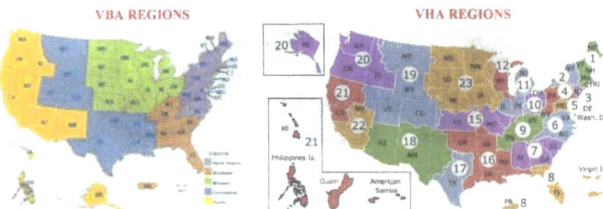

It is imperative to maintain the health of both Active Duty and Reservists. Dental Class 3 and Class 4 are the military's greatest problem in Readiness. With Reserve Recalls dentistry is often needed before In-Country Deployment resulting in Delayed Response times when maximum Total Force efficiency is required. Full Command Structure upon DoD determination.

Restructuring DoD into VA for Humanitarian and National Emergencies

a) Restructure Non-Combat Geneva Convention Code assets into DoD war time functions for each Branch of Service.

b) DoD as well as Each Branch of Service may have upon determination the ability to issue Stand-By Orders as they see fit to emergent situations within their scope of function and interests therein. Seriousness and Heads-Up may be within a Coded Seriousness of potential Threat. FUNCTIONAL SCENERIO: Hurricane Katrina.

c) Reserve Military Assets includes all Support Functions to make Command and Control fluid and timely. LOGISTICS.

d) AIR FORCE and USPHS: VA Hospitals function as a Rear Echelon Fleet Hospital. **1)** Command and Control belongs to the Air Force. **2)** Administrative functions for all Branched of Services are to be Deployed to the VA Hospital. **3)** Orders are to be written while assets are Deployed as when 9/11 occurred one of our New York FORCEMED (USMC) Units IMMEDIATELY went to the scene. **4)** VA and Medical Schools to assist.

e) ARMY functions as a MASH Element and should be Deployed to VA Clinics outside immediate Hospital access and/or Triage assessed for Medical Evacuation to the VA Hospital/Fleet Hospital.

f) NAVY functions where most needed whether at the VA Fleet Hospital, VA Clinic MASH scenario AND USMC Attached FORCEMED First Responder in highly most mobile BATTALION AID STATIONS.

g) ALL AIR ASSETS and MOTOR TRANSPORT Reserve Components function according to Branch of Service and/or where needed. This includes AIR NATIONAL GUARD.

h) SECURITY Presence as determined by each Branch of Service, DoD, Joint Chiefs command decisions.

i) RESULT: **1)** Purpose and Function Maximized. **2)** DoD secures PRIMARY use of their Assets before other Agencies as DHS and the IRS. **3)** Civilian Assets will volunteer.

EXTERNAL CIVIL INTEGRATION

Veterans who rate a disability should be given Tricare for Life and allowed to seek civilian health care if more expedient and as a Supplemental Insurance to Social Security Disability. All Veterans should automatically be given Tricare for Life when they turn 65, the current retirement age as a Supplemental secondary insurance to Social Security.

Being Tricare is a DoD government insurance program other branches of our government should be allowed to use and participate in its benefits. Administration for other than DoD use would best be through Department of Health and Human Services (DHHS) and be as a replacement for many instead of Obamacare. The premium rates would be far less. The vetted Obamacare insurance companies are the same as the insurance companies lost by many due to Obamacare, and the insurance company's profits are higher with Obamacare. The program exists, web site up and running and all that would be necessary is to use their existing Family Plans to choose from and put a Code Number for the coverage program just as any other insurance coverage identification clarification.

By using Tricare through DHHS instead of Obamacare it will transfer Administration of Health Care away from Department of Homeland Security (DHS) and the Internal Revenue Service (IRS) and put any form of National Health Care where it belongs, to put in other words, health care should be run by health care professionals.

It all depends on what society truly desires in health care. By using Tricare instead of Obamacare eliminated would, **in part**, be:

a) Elimination of the Death Penalty clause where people are paying for executions.
b) More appropriately eliminate the possibility of the Saudi invention of a Wifi activated Lethal Dose in the soon to be required computer chip.
c) Reduce politically favored exemptions as well as contractual fraud.
d) Eliminate stagnation of treatment to allow industry standards of treatment updates which is how Tricare is set up to do.

VA EMPLOYEE and CONTRACTOR UCMJ ACCOUNTABILITY

10 U.S. CODE CHAPTER 47: UCMJ

ALL employees of Veterans Affairs who have ever served in any Branch of the United States Uniformed Services are still under the Uniform Code of Military Justice (UCMJ) and subject to recall for non-judicial punishment. This includes the very probable loss of Benefits and Retirement Pay if applicable. Included in this are those who are NOT Veterans Affairs employees but Health Care Providers who while in the military performed illicit medical studies of a criminal nature that leads to improper medical care and the disciplining of those who object to their improper use of medicine. This includes VA patients.

The VA is supporting medical procedures that may become a part of PTSD through the causation of Alexithymia. To deepen VA culpability the very social structure also, besides the very medical procedure that causes actual brain changes, may cause Alexithymia.

Two sections of the UCMJ that they may be prosecuted under include, in part, Article 2 and Article 15. They state, **in part**:

10 U.S. CODE § 802 - ARTICLE 2 UCMJ

a) Retired members of a regular component of the Armed Forces who are entitled to retirement pay are subject to the provisions of the UCMJ. . . and may be tried to court-martial for violations of the UCMJ that occurred while they were on active duty or while in a retired status.
b) Retired Reserve Component Soldiers are subject to recall to active duty for the investigation of UCMJ offenses they are alleged to have committed while in Title 10 status, for trial by court-martial, or for proceedings under UCMJ, Article 15.

ARTICLE 15 UCMJ

a) Forfeitures imposed under the UCMJ, Article 15 may even be applied against retirement pay.

V: VA Infantilization of Veterans

He found himself envying people who are protected by the maternal embrace of an organization. **Marie Louise von Franz.[1]**

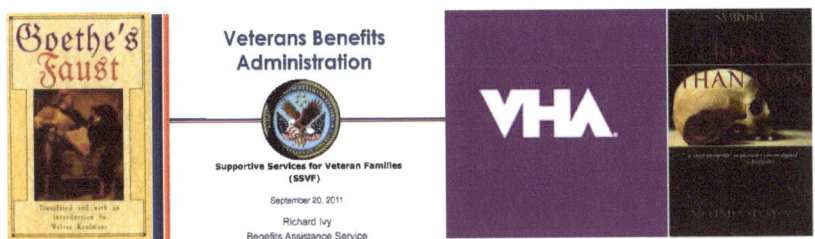

Before learning what pathology looks like, a surgeon must know what normal tissues look like. Same with psychic factors including *psychosexuality*. When behaviors become ritualistic from the individual, organizational or national the same applies.

Unlike Freud and others who concentrated much of their work on the abnormal Maslow developed the Hierarchy of Needs by studying exemplary people and students finding a 5 Step Pattern of Behavior that can be studied Forensically to an Appearance of Normalcy. *Behavior reflects personality.*[2]

Maslow found when one level of growth in life's endeavor both physical and psychic, becomes reasonably fulfilled they begin reaching upward. To the opposite, as loss of pay, benefits withheld or taken away, rapid progression downward may occur.[3-4] Such is the case of veteran treatment by the VA:

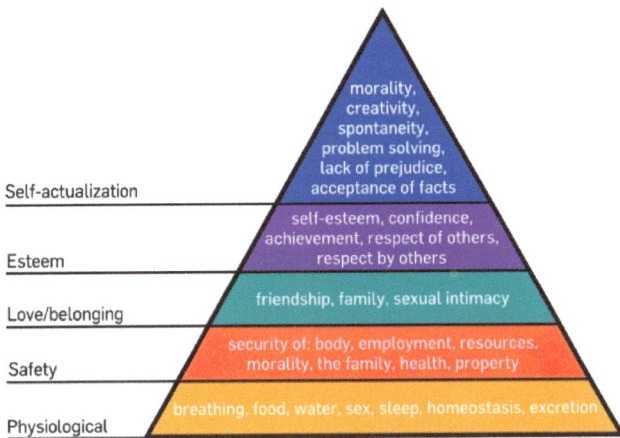

PHYSIOLOGICAL

Physiological Needs are primary, most primal and essential for Life. Physiological Needs include such factors as: food, water, air, homeostasis, air-oxygen, activity, rest, sleep avoidance of pain – Pleasure Principle, sex and creation and species continuity.

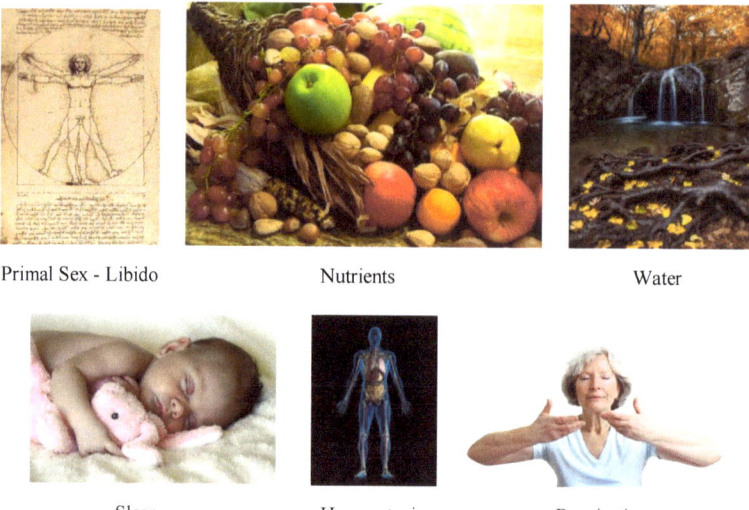

| Primal Sex - Libido | Nutrients | Water |

| Sleep | Homeostasis | Respiration |

Physiological Needs are closest to Instinctual drives to stay alive. As well, they are most tied to the unconscious Freudian id. Without these basic functions self and species will perish. The id lies deep in the Archetypic Dimension; whereas, explanations belong to the Mythic Expression. Freud used myth in naming the Life principle as Greek child god Eros – Roman Cupid and Thanatos the Greek child god of Death – Roman Mors. Thanatos enshrines the Death Wish. The result is Games of Death.

So, who is the Wild Woman? She is the Life/Death/Life force... the incubator. Clarissa Pinkola Estes.[5]

Pleasure Principle: (German: Lustprinzip) is the instinctual seeking of pleasure and avoiding pain in order to satisfy biological and psychological needs.[6] Specifically, the pleasure principle is the driving force guiding the id.[7] Self Preservation.

Thanatos (Greek: To die, be dying) is the Death Wish, in fear of death and change often results in rituals of Transformation using the Life/Death/Life motif. He exists with Hades in the Underworld. Siblings include: Geras (old Age), Oizys (Suffering), Moros (doom), Apate (Deception), Momus (Blame), Eris (strife), Nemesis (Retribution) along with the boatman to Hades Charon. He is associated with the Hesiod goddesses that are the Moirai including Atropos (Death goddess in her own right and Keres (violent death). Euthanasia is Greek for a Good Death. Loosely as Children of the Darkness they associate with the Mesopotamian Ugarti goddesses Lilith, specifically the Night Children of the Biblical Screech Owl Lilith known as the Lilim(n) with, in some variants, Mesopotamian Samael her husband Angel of Death.

SAFETY

After Physiological Needs are reasonably met, next focus of attention centers mostly on Safety and Security concerns. Safety and Security Needs involve natural desires for stability, limits, structured living conditions law and order.

Shelter

Safe Surroundings - Work - Play

Law & Order - Boundaries

Resources - Property

Family

Structural Living

Lloyd deMause outlined 6 basic steps in the Evolution of Child-rearing Practices. The result of Physiological Needs is represented by victim *suicide* from more abuse that the individual can accrue. They are:[8] 1a): Early Infanticidal Mode; 1b): Late Infanticidal Mode; 2): Abandoning Mode; 3): Ambivalent Mode; 4): Intrusive Mode; 5): Socializing Mode; and, 6): Helping Mode. These steps also highly correlate to social integration.[9] The first 3 apply here:

1a): Early Infanticidal Mode occurs mainly in small kinship groups. The mothers used their children as symbols of poison containment and the killing represents purification.

1b): Late Infanticidal Mode evolves as societies become more complex. The poison container theory is kept, and the earth mother goddess became the most common medium in child sacrifice. The excuse of satisfying the gods relates to the internalized parents: (Jungian Mana Family triad communicating within Transactional Analysis illustrated in Mythic Expression emanating from the id's Archetypic Dimension).

2): The Abandoning Mode sacrifices in procedures as exposure instead of actual killing. Reasons may include birth defects to a perception common in Angels of Death that the victim does not have the right to live. (This is akin to death under denial of Physiological Needs, but the choice to do so resides in this stage of Maslow's growth and development. Spartans exposed physically inferior infants on a rock to die.)

3): The Ambivalent Mode tolerates love-hate feelings and actions without connecting the differences between them. (The improper use of Power, Control and Assumed Authority may enhance this Modus Operandi by just using all available resources to build walls through Operating Procedures that ignore and debilitate victim success in proper *contracted* survival.)

LOVE/BELONGING

After both of the previous more basic Needs are met to varying satisfaction the nest stage of our growth and development involves closeness with affection: friendship, spouse, children, extended family and sexual intimacy. We, gregarious humanity, need community.

| Friendship | Pair Bonding | Intimacy |

| Extended Family | Best Friends Forever | Always - Faithful |

deMause's Third level in the Evolution of Child-rearing Practices is loosely observable to the societal growth and development of Veteran Affairs organized criminal behavior:

4): The Intrusive Mode establishes child abuse within the frame-working of discipline. (Ritual enters. All rituals represent Nature vs. Humanity by recognizing our inherent violence. Rituals manipulate objects, including those humans deemed improper in existence, and are rooted in Thanatos mock-death motifs as the Catholic Mass, the death of Jesus.)

Chris Knight in *Blood Relations* taught:[10]

Clan solidarity – always split or cut across the biological family, since a husband would always belong to and over his primary loyalties to one clan while his wife and children belonged to another... Engels insisted that it was vital to an understanding of human history and prehistory to accept this priority of the unilineal clan over 'the family.' In the beginning, marriage as modern Europeans understand this term was unknown. A husband acquired neither unconditional property rights in nor authority over his wife and her children. Instead, a man's kinship rights were in his sister and her children, just as his shared in property were rights in the resources of his own matrilineal clan, not his wife's... The message of the myth was clear. In the beginning, women were superior to men.

Regarding sexual opposites Harriet Rubin theorized:

The first law of the Princessa is to become a woman who combines opposites... Change the rules and you are playing your game... She who is governed by principles, not laws, is undeterred.[11]

ESTEEM

There are two forms of Esteem. Self-esteem and Esteem from others. Self-esteem carries feelings of confidence, competence, achievement, mastery, interdependence, and freedom. The other is esteem and respect from others as status, fame, glory, recognition, attention, reputation, appreciation, even dominance.

Dominance   Respect from Others - Adulation - Deification   R: improper Self-esteem

Accomplishment, Mastery, Freedom   Self Respect   Family (Community) Respect and Honoring

deMause's fifth Evolution of Child-rearing Practices is:

5): The Socializing Mode occurs where the mother is perceived the perfect parent and the male family provider being the family provider. (This is our current system at its social highest and yet a denial ingrains regarding th12e feminine Dark Side which can, and often does, creep into any social system).

Pedagogy is the art and science of indoctrinating children. Alice Miller illustrated **Poisonous Pedagogy** with these essential elements:[12]

1): Adults are the masters (not the servants) of the dependent child.

2): They determine in godlike fashion what is right and what is wrong.

3): The child is held responsible for parental anger.

4): The parents must always be shielded.

5): The child's life-affirming feelings pose a threat to autocratic adults.

6): The child must be "broken" as soon as possible.

7): Procedures are performed so victim will 'not notice' and expose the perpetrator.

SELF-ACTUALIZATION

Self-Actualization is the satisfactory feeling of achieving the top of the ladder where that person has become what and where they feel they ought to be. Self-Actualization should involve morality, creativity, spontaneity, problem solving, lack of prejudice, acceptance of facts. Life's endeavor fulfilled.

Morality – Lack of Prejudice   Spontaneity   Fulfillment

Creativity   Problem Solving   Fact Acceptance – Ah-Ha

The **Conundrum of Self-Actualization** is once achieved it must be maintained, or a new subject taken on starting lower on the Needs pyramid. Musician at the top of their profession most often than not will continue to make music. Sport Champions continue their game. *Cultural VA waiting times continue.*

Repetition Compulsion (*Wiederholungszwang*) is *Maladaptive* behavior that repeats. Despite efforts to the contrary Repetition Compulsion does not achieve Mastery and rarely resolves without psychotherapy. Recent studies propose into two causes. First, Non-Traumatic origin; and, Second, Traumatic origin brought forth by Freud. Overlap may occur. Repetitive Maladaptive behavior of non-traumatic origin arises from an **evolutionary** process where Patterns of Behavior frequently displayed by **caregivers**, and compatible with **child's temperament** are acquired, maintained and repeated. Familiarity with ego-syntonic aspects strongly Motivate the person to retain the behavior. Repetitive Maladaptive Behavior of traumatic origin is characterized by Defensive **Dissociation** of both the **Cognitive and Emotional** components of trauma making it difficult to integrate the experience and thus help overcome the Improper Behavior. The strong resistance of Maladaptive Behavior to change is based on the influence of both types of origin on the personality, and to many variables. Dissociation may lead to a Punitive Personality Disorder.[13]

Borderline Personality Disorder (BPD) is a pattern of abnormal behavior characterized by extreme fear of **abandonment**, **unstable relationships with other people**, **sense of self**, or **emotions**, **feelings of emptiness**; and, **frequent dangerous behaviors**; symptoms may be triggered by seemingly normal events; as well as, in twin studies the illness is partly inherited from one's parents and possibly coupled with environmental components; along with traits as impulsiveness and aggression that can be attributed to **temperament**.[14] People with BPD, *more often seen in females*, engage in **idealization** and *devaluation* of others and thus assumed to be the person's **intention**.[15] There is evidence that abnormalities of the *frontolimbic* networks are associated with many of the symptoms.[16] ***Being frontolimbic there is high correlation to psychosexuality.***

PHYSIOLOGICAL PSYCHOSEXUAL RELATIONS

The woman becomes the vehicle of nature.
The man becomes the vehicle society, the social order, the social purpose.
The woman is life. The man is the servant of life...
Life has overtaken her. Woman is what it is all about,
the giving of birth and the giving of nourishment.
Without him she would be overwhelmed.
Joseph Campbell, *The Power of Myth*.

Psychosexual Ethos

According to Solomon: *Rather than thinking of ethics in terms of impersonal, abstract, moral principles of right and wrong claimed Gillian, women tend to think of ethics in terms of moral personal responsibility. While men understood a moral dilemma posed by the experimenter as a problem of right and wrong answer, women understood such a dilemma as a result of an interpersonal conflict in need of a resolution, not a right-versus-wrong answer. Gillian hypothesized that in addition to the moral reasoning grounded in abstract principles of right and wrong by Kant and Kolhberg, there is also a 'feminine' but equally valid type of moral reasoning that is grounded in maintaining the stability of interpersonal relationships... The feminine 'ethics of care' is a superior, more mature type of moral reasoning than that which appeals to abstract ideas.*[17]

Immanuel Kant

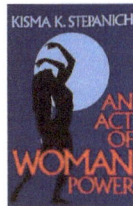

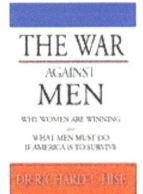

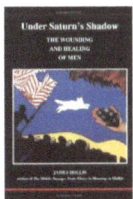

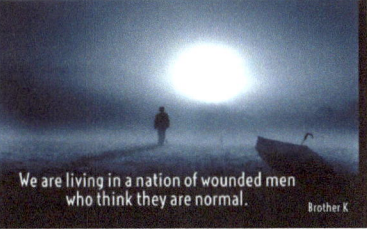
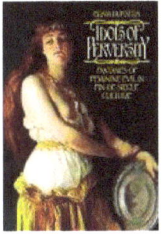

Spirituality is; Theology explains; Religion practices.[18] The imago is an idealized mental image of someone. It is usually a parent that influences a person's behavior. Deity-human connection is through the imago Dei meaning "image of God." Edward Edinger described the ***imago Dei*** as:[19]

The Self is the ordering and unifying center of the total psyche (conscious and unconscious) just as the ego is the center of the conscious personality. Or, put in other words, the ego is the seat of the subjective identity while the Self is the seat of the objective identity. The Self is thus the supreme psychic authority and subordinates the ego to it. The Self is most simply described as the inner empirical deity and is identical with the imago Dei.

Freud's **Reality Principle** (*Realitatsprinzip*) is the capacity for Deferred Gratification when reality disallows its immediate gratification as best. It represents growth of the ego out of the id. Maturity by leaving the id of immediate gratification. It is acceptance of pleasure postponed and sometimes diminished due to seeking only selfishness without responsibility including seeking sex.[20] Next to function thusly is of the super-ego, social. deMause's final Evolution of Child-rearing Practices is:

6): The Helping Mode removes conditions of violation.

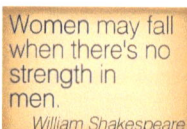   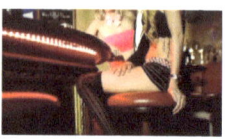

All are culpable in a **Conspiracy**. Militarily, as the VA is not coupled with the DoD is to be considered as if a **Mutiny**. The VA collectively imposes an **Undue Burden** on Veterans:[21]

(1): BURDEN generally, anything that is grievous, wearisome, or oppressive. 297 S,W, 2d 39, 44.
(2): BURDEN OF PROOF the duty of a party to substantiate an **allegation** or **issue** either to avoid the **dismissal** of that issue early in the trial or in order to convince the 'trier of facts" as to the truth of that claim and hence to prevail in a criminal suit.

Thus, **by convention feminine Cultural Relativity usurps masculine empiric Rule of Law.**

ORGANIZATIONAL

IT IS EASIER TO PUNISH THE COMPLIANT[22]

  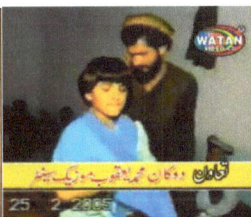  

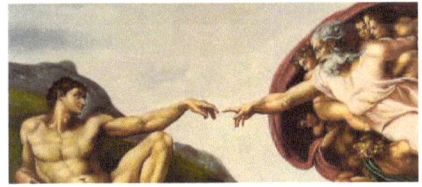 

LIFE   **DEATH**

 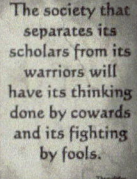 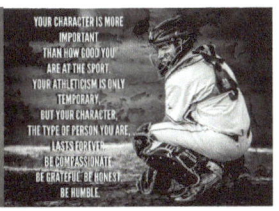

GLEN A. COSTIE

Medicine has only usurped the shaman as primitive societies diminish.[23] The process of Passive Initiation, having others do something for them. This has also been correlated by FBI Profilers regarding certain aspects of Team Predation.[24] The social structure is discussed by Baker in *Reclaiming the Dark Goddess*.[25]

In mythology, desire is associated with the feminine principle, and desire in any human being. Traditional cultures control desire through ritual... Indigenous people know well that if life-force energy is not contained in some way, it can become an out-of-control, intrusive, destructive thing... Traditional cultures control desire through ritual... The feminine carries the desire, and the masculine goes forth to fulfill it.

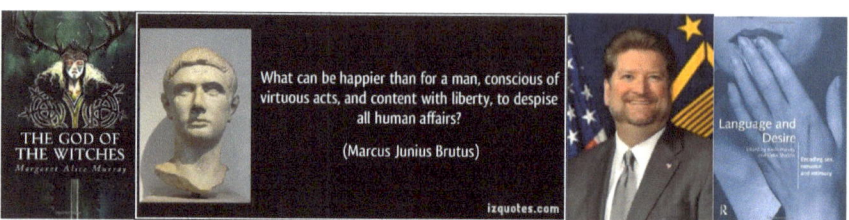

Glen A. Costie is the Dayton, Ohio VA Medical Director and a member of the Senior Executives Association.[26] They aid VA senior executives for court proceedings for the AFGE. Membership is NOT VA limited. Their reach is deep.

DAVID COX

Theory is immersed in theological and medical error based in the power of the Wild Woman in her Life/Death/Life cycle.[27] Her function includes social instruction and maintainer of tradition.[28] Through ritual one must take their original existence through a make believe death ritual to enter the Proper Social Order.[29] The social avenue is discussed by Knight in *Blood Relations* with:[30]

Human symbolic structure emerged out of struggle. Its rituals and myths were expressions of 'counterdominance' – signals for thwarting exploitation by males. The Signalers were female, allied with their male kin; their targets were mates.

David Cox is President of the AFGE. When VA Secretary McDonald pleaded with Congress to be allowed to fire employees he stated he would '*whoop ass*' Secretary McDonald as well as calling Gen, McDonald a *fool*.[31] Media Internet hush. I do not cite You Tube.

EUGENE HUDSON

Carol Meyers in *Discovering Eve* wrote:[32]

Both men and women will tend to perpetrate a system of social balance; of male authority offset by female power... Women may exert their will and prevail over male members of society in ways that are of consequence for all members of society. Yet the formal configurations of the society might easily give the appearance that males dominate. In other words, overt cultural patterns may accord prestige to males rather than females, but social reality may present a different picture.

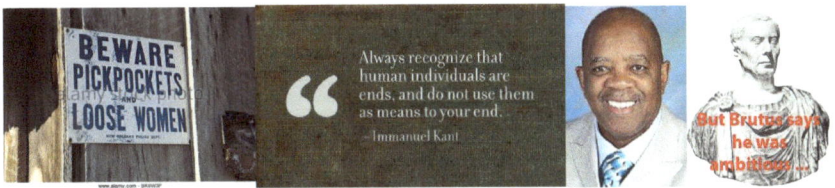

Eugene Hudson is Secretary-Treasurer of the AFGE.[33]

AUGUSTA THOMAS

Functional structure is as if the Matriarchy of Society. Put otherwise this structure is termed The Great Round[34] as well as the Center.[35] She is the **life** force, giver-**taker**. Thus, in social death motif, ritual, ***the child experiences the socialized apocalyptic event***,[36] and with the VA the psychologized Child is the Veteran. Shulamith Firestone's Gender Feminism argued:[37]

This gut reaction – the assumption that, even when they don't know it, feminists are talking about changing a fundamental biological condition. The goals of feminism can never be achieved by evolution, but only through revolution.

Augusta Thomas is in charge of the AFGE Fair Practice department. *Discovering Eve* Meyers noted: [38]

Authority is a hierarchical arrangement that may be expressed in formal legal or juridical traditions. Power has no such cultural sanctions but nonetheless plays a decisive role in social interactions... Men, on fact wielded very little power. Male dominance is thus a public attitude of deference or of theoretical control but not a valid description of social reality... Women's power is culturally muted but functionally active.

ELIZABETH JOYCE FREEMAN

Chris Knight in *Blood Relations: Menstruation and the Origins of Culture* noted:[39]

Menstrual blood is in virtually all mythologies associated with (a) moon and (b) blood from a wound. In hunting symbolism, wounds and bleeding vaginas are frequently juxtaposed, and the one blood may be thought to promote the flowing of the other.

With totemism the mother's matrilineal blood and the animal's blood equates as one generational flesh, is divine, and is of god and divine power... The blood of one's mother and her matrilineal clan is identified with the blood of an animal selected as the clan's emblem. The clan members consider themselves as a single flesh, 'a single meat,' a single blood, and this flesh is that of the mythical being from whom all have descended.

Within the shared blood resides the 'god' or 'totem' of the clan, from it follows that the blood is a divine thing – inseparable from menstrual and other blood... The potencies associated with sacrificial or other blood have for millennia meshed closely and sometimes indistinguishly with notions 'divine power.'

The message was clear. In the beginning, woman was superior to men.

   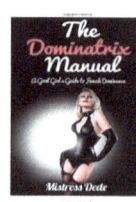 

Elizabeth Joyce Freeman is the VA Western Regions disciplinarian. Put in other words she is the go to VA ***Hit Man*** whether it be a Pharmacy Tech noting a system error, improperly treated patient demanding proper treatment or all the way to the top, a: Whistleblower.[40]

Native American societies were and are matriarchal. Sharon Burch related the following Navaho myth-working legend:[41]

One day a man went hunting for deer while the woman stayed home to garden, cook and weave. Returning from a very long and tiring hunt, the man brought back a fat deer that he had killed. He felt very proud of himself. The woman made a very stew of the meat and they enjoyed the bountiful meal. When they had finished eating, the woman wiped her greasy hands on her dress, belched and said, "Thank you my vagina." After hearing what the woman said, the man asked, "What is it that you said?" She repeated what she said. "Why do you speak in this manner?" he asked. Was it not I who killed the deer – whose flesh you have eaten? Why do you not thank me? Was it your vagina that killed the deer?" "Yes," she replied. "My vagina is a great hunter. If it were not for that, you would not have killed the deer. It is for want of that you men hunt and bring food to us women. It is my vagina that does all the work." The story continues with the man and the woman getting into an argument and separating. Then one day, Owl paid a visit and reminded the man about continuing the growth of the people. After thinking about it, he saw the wisdom of the Owl and admitted how desperately he had missed the woman.

I grew up knowing that woman was the strong one – the life giver. The Navaho have reverence and respect for women because of that... Men know they are there to help with procreation and to assist women. That is how it is... We never question that... Growing up, I never knew that other cultures weren't matriarchal. My grandfather told me, "You are what your mother is."

PRITZ (Navara) NAVARATNASINGAM

Matriarchal and Patriarchal functions cannot exist without the other. The VA uses societal play mock death rituals.[42] John Douglas profiled:[43]

Serial killers are inadequate types to begin with, and the ones who need partners to carry out their work are the most inadequate of all.

Pritz "Navara" as he signed his name Oakland, CA during contention of not paying VBA benefits owed as back pay in relation to MetLife is tied into a greater Conspiracy among VCA and Insurance companies. After 3 years of begging the veteran issued a Dr.'s Mandated Report to San Francisco Region appropriate DOJ office. It took a Mandated Report just 3 weeks for the Dr, Veteran to receive his back-pay Disability as he is rated. BUT the veteran lost 4 years of his *Supplemental* Disability Insurance provided by his employer California Indian Health due to MetLife's one-year notification policy for submittal of all other disability benefits received. At that time there were rumors of veterans being granted disability, told they were denied, and the funds put in secret bank accounts.

From Oakland BVA Pritz went to head Houston VA and was involved in the Waiting List scandal. Next is now Director of Seattle, Washington VA. He replaced Julianna Boor in Seattle and in return Ms. Boor took over Oakland VBA. A circle has been completed.[44-45]

LAURA H. ESKENAZI

Regarding moods and motivations, Bell stated:[46]

Ritual emerges as a means for a provisional synthesis of some form of original opposition... Such dispositions are, in turn, further differentiated into two kinds: moods and motivations... Yet something else may well be at work when ritual is to be declared The Basic Social Act.

  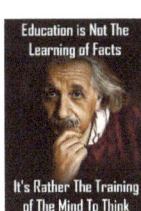  

Laura Eskenazi is Executive-in-Charge and Vice Chairman of the VA Board of Appeals. She is among the top 10% pay scale with an ES00 rating. With reply statements issuing further review with the original VBA Regional office, her office sends files back to the wrong Regions for stated reviews, but actually to bury the veteran further for however long it takes the veteran to discover the impropriety.[47]

SHIELA M. CULLEN

Shiela Cullen Fraudently reported on her VA Application for Employment that she possesses a Masters Degree which she does not possess.[48] She is now Network Director, VA Sierra Pacific Network (VISN 21). Union contracts and internal criminality prohibits proper results. VA Secretary McDonald is prohibited from firing her and others, acknowledging there is a leadership crisis within the VA.[49]

The LIE
Sir Walter Raleigh

Go, Soul, the body's guest,
Upon a thankless arrant:
Fear not to touch the best;
The truth shall be thy warrant:
Go, since I must die,
And give the world the lie.

Say to the court it glows
And shines like rotten wood;
Say to the church, it shows
What's good, and doth no good:
If church and court reply,
Then give them both the lie.

Tell potentates, they live
Acting by others' action,
Not loved unless they give,
Not strong but by faction:
If potentates reply,
Give potentates the lie.

Tell men of high condition
That manage the estate,
Their purpose is ambition,
Their practice only hate;
And if they make reply,
Then give them all the lie.

Tell them that brave it most,
They beg for more by spending,
Who, in their greatest cost,
Seek nothing but commending:
And if they reply,
Then give them all the lie.

Tell zeal it wants devotion;
Tell love it is but lust;
Tell time it is but motion;
Tell flesh it is but dust:
And wish them not reply,
For thou must give the lie.

Tell age it daily wasteth;
Tell honor how it alters;
Tell beauty how she blasteth;
Tell favor how she falters:
And as they shall reply,
Then give everyone the lie.

Tell wit how much it wrangles
In tickle points of niceness;
Tell wisdom she entangles
Herself in over-wiseness:
And when they do reply,
Straight give them both the lie.

Tell physic of her boldness;
Tell skill it is pretension;
Tell charity of coldness;
Tell law it is contention:

And as they do reply,
So give them still the lie.

Tell fortune of her blindness;
Tell nature of decay;
Tell friendship of unkindness;
Tell justice of delay:
And if they will reply,
Then give them all the lie.

Tell arts they have no soundness,
But vary by esteeming;
Tell schools they want profoundness,
And stand too much on seeming:
If arts and school reply,
Give arts and school the lie.

Tell faith it fled the city;
Tell how the country erreth;
Tell manhood shakes off pity;
Tell virtue least preferreth:
And if they do reply,
Spare not to give the lie.

So when thou hast, as I
Commanded thee, done blabbing, --
Although to give the lie
Deserves no less than stabbing, --
Stab at thee, he that will,
No stab the soul can kill.

JULIANNA BOOR

Matriarchal and Patriarchal functions cannot exist without the other. The VA uses societal play mock death rituals.[50] Bell noted:[51]

Ritualization is central to culture as the means to dominate nature and the natural violence within human beings. Although ritual (=culture) is the necessary repression of this violence (=nature), culture is still dependent upon the energy of aggression as well as its restraints... Ritual structure is totally repressive; instead of channeling violence, the order of ritual completely denies it.

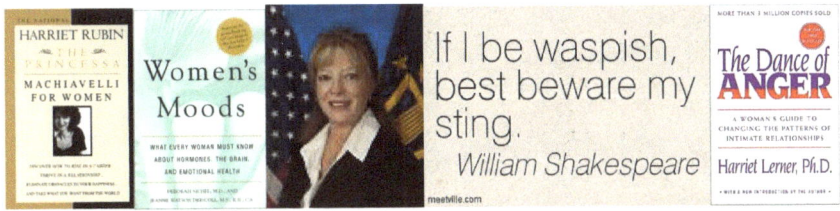

Julianna Boor became Director Oakland VBA. When this case was brought to her attention she miraculously found what Pritz with Ricky Young and Ulrike Willimon refused to give the veteran, and sent the veteran an UNNAMED and UNSIGNED notification putting the veteran in court with the statement to the effect: *What do you think about that*. It was found that 13,184 claim were stashed in a cabinet with no required action taken. Testimony stated some files were duplicates. Even so the case in 11 years was never adjudicated other than sending to Phoenix where the misdiagnosed veteran would die of cancer and neatly eliminated altogether[52] This occurs with multi-disciplinary files that inhibit bonuses.

MICHELE M. KWOK

Mircea Elaide stated.[53]

Reality is acquired solely through repetition or participation, everything else lacks an exemplary model is 'meaningless,' i.e. it lacks reality.

Michele transferred from Los Angeles Regional Office as Veterans Service Center Manager to become Assistant Director of the Oakland Regional Benefit Office. She has now reached the Mother aspect within female spirituality from Princess on her way to a Dark Side Hag-Witch instead of what her true feminine role should be as a Light Side Crone-Wise Woman. Her apogee of existence.[54]

DIANA RUBENS – KIMBERLY GRAVES

De River in *The Sexual Criminal: A Psychoanalytical Study* revealed:[55]

The motives for the offense may be many, and the sentiments from which they spring innumerable. There is usually slow inner tension which produces an outburst of willed cruel acts which have been carefully thought out and planned as to details. In a great many cases the female sadistic criminal uses her paramour as an accomplice in carrying out crimes of hideous and violent nature. Through her cunning persuasion she induces her lover to murder those whom she wants to get rid of. She is lacking in affect towards mankind, in fact towards humanity in general; yet she is clever enough to convince her sexual partner of love and to entice him to enter into a pact with her to carry out the crime.

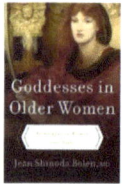    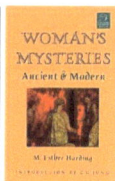

CDR Robert Harger, SEAL, after being first in post Pol Pot Cambodia noted.[56]

The problem with genocide is it turns in on itself.

Rubens and Graves arranged to receive transfers to lesser responsible positions while retaining same pay and expensive moving costs. The VA tries to rotate senior executives in five year cycles. The discrepancy is Rubens and Graves selected employment positions choice for them and the two replaced employees were not scheduled to rotate and forced to abandon their positions and take other positions elsewhere.

RESOLUTION

The person who granted the positions was a retired USAF General from the health professions and familiar with military protocol. Being the VA is integrating with DoD it would possibly be appropriate to open the military available solution. The **Twilight Tour**.

MILERSMAN 1300-600; CH-36, 30 Aug 2011 is the Navy's Twilight Tours Directive. Requests are for the last tour before a 30-year retirement. Primary choice is a location by Region, then which bases. Navy needs come first and Sea Duty is preferred assignment if open. This allows for future family stability and the service member to seek future employment. It is a good management tool.

And, yet through it all, Douglas with Olshaker's extensive Profiling concluded:[57]

So let's get this straight and state it plainly: It is my belief, based on several decades of experience, study, and analysis, that the overwhelming majority of repeat sexual predators do what they do because they want to, because it gives them a satisfaction they do not achieve in any other aspect of their lives, and because it makes them feel good, regardless of the consequences to others. In that respect, the crime represents the ultimate in selfishness; the perpetrator doesn't care what happens to his victim as long as he gets what he wants. In fact, exercising this manipulation, domination, and control – and the infliction of pain and death are for him their ultimate expressions – are the critical factors in making him feel complete and fully alive.

CATHERINE MITRANO

Dr. Catherine Bell emphasized:[58]

Any ritual performance must be based on and legitimized by the 'superior authority;... In the fixity of ritual's structure lies the prestige of tradition and in this prestige lies its power.., formalization effectively determines content, transforming the specific into the general terms of a natural and preexisting order.., formalization not only produces a form of authority, 'traditional authority,' rooted in the appeal to the past.., formality puts people in a situation that discourages challenge and compels acceptance.

Catherine Mitrano is Director VA Resolution Board. Twice over a year ago other OIGs have written her stating she needs to resolve the case this Mandated Report's case. Therefore, this Enclosure is a part of the continuing updating. All these VA rituals, individually and grouped, are forms of ***worshipping the dead*** they killed, their creations, through actuality in some category of Homicide, through *Thanatos* or both and charging the House of Worship.[59] "Behold! My creation lives," *Frankenstein.*

SISTERHOOD – ET AL.

Douglas and Olshaker in *Obsession* Criminally Profiled that:[60]

When you've analyzed what should be the motive based on the crime scenario and that doesn't make sense, and you go through all other "logical" ones and you can't make one of them fit reasonably, then you start looking into psychiatric territory. All crimes have a motive; all crimes make sense according to some logic, though that logic may be a strictly internal one with no relationship to any "objective: logic. In many instances, a hidden sexual motive emerges, a motive that originates in fantasy.

Gina Farrisee, Assistant Secretary Office of Human Resources and Administration; Leigh Bradley, Office of General Council Department of Veterans Affairs; and, LaVerne Council, Chief Information Officer. In CIRCULARITY most of these positions cover-up for the mistakes big enough for their attention. This circularity is more amenable to feminine communications, ritual's circularity and the illicit computer program to bypass improprieties back to originating individuals.

CHERYL A. POIRRIER

The veteran is reduced to child status. The younger the child the easier. De River observed:[61]

Women may far surpass the male in refined, planned cruelty and acts of perversity.

Refused to treat VA patient who fell from his wheel chair, then Falsified VA patient Medical Records regarding the patient's death.[62] The younger the child the more likely a female perpetrator.

GERMAINE CLARNO

Organized Sociopathy in Major Sadism has become a *VA Social Norm*.[63]

Was it Public Relations you did for the Gestapo, or Community Relations?

Ms. Clarno and Union officials let VA patients die so not to talk with Republicans.[64]

CYNTHIA TANNER

Patterns of Behavior are worldly even in England.[65]

Once you give up your integrity, the rest is a piece of cake.

Ms. Tanner embezzled $830,000 from a veterans charity.[66]

JOHN WOODITCH - MASTURBATOR

Douglas and Olshaker in *Obsession* continued to Criminally Profiled that:[67]

Tragically this motive of uncontrolled anger and the need for sexual domination doesn't always occur against strangers. Many sexual sadists are married or in ongoing relationships – totally self-involved narcissists.

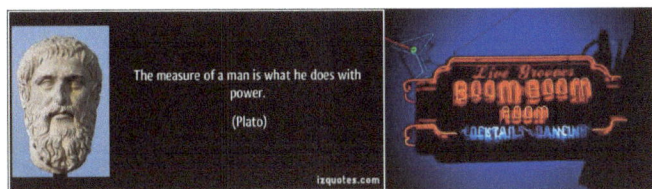

John Wooditch was VAOIG acting Deputy Inspector General. In 2003 he was reprimanded for pornography on his office computer. Later Wooditch frequented the office all glass conference room to masturbate and seen by fellow employees and others visiting. He was allowed to retire.[68] More likely than not he never belonged to The Gilgal Society of the pediatricians and other professors at Universities of San Francisco, Johns Hopkins or University of Sydney that is a group effort in that behavior with their own published pornography and erotica contained in a book for a previous VA-OSHA Mandated Report. As Michel Jackson in the vernacular made the girls swoon with: ¶Just Beat It.¶

WES MORRELL, MONTEREY COUNTY, CA

Similar to Red Flagging and other VA procedures, former Gestapo officer K Lindeau officer testified in the Nuremburg Trials that.[69]

These teams were assigned to the camp commandant and had the job to segregate the prisoners of war who were candidates for execution, according to the orders that had been given, and to report them to the office police.

The common conundrum for Mr. Morrell is he took a medical discussion as a Representative from VA Oakland Region that was directly opposite performed tests and diagnosis and acted on it. Included was the statement to disregard the letter from Congressman Sam Farr. Liability lies with the County, which, in turn, passes to the VA. HIPPA violations apply to both State and Federal Agencies.[70]

One must understand the discourse of this case's Criminal Reports regarding the Jungian feminine and masculine principles as they relate to the Eastern Yin and Yang from which Carl Jung named the Anima and Animus that were eventually developed further by his wife Emma Jung and students in the vein of Marie Louise von Franz through to including Clarissa Pinkola Estes. Douglas with Olshaker Profiled.[71]

This is nothing but elementary butchery. And we have long since learned that serial killers need nothing but will to commit whatever atrocities they want on a body... They are willing to have someone else die for their selfish purposes, and that is one of the definitions of sociopathic behavior.., based on my research and experience, there is no possibility of rehabilitating this type of individual. If he is ever let out, he will kill again.

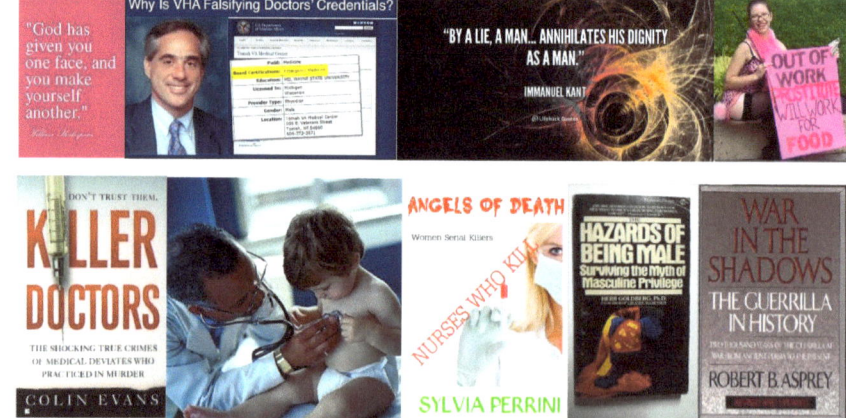

The VA is rife with using professionals in improper positions, without proper licenses, violations of pharmaceuticals, fiving incomplete care that may kill patients – and the list grows longer and longer.[72] ¶And the beat goes on.¶

The victim is a <u>representation</u>. It is as if the American President represents the United States society, and the male child represents the masculine. The intellectual overlay, especially to the Organized type is a cause.

The cause used as an excuse is a convenient justification. It is transference in Reason Avoidance so not to confront and deal with reality. There is often a dissociation of the perpetrator's parental figure to the same sex of the victim. The violent act is from a deep seated inadequacy. To solve the problem of inadequacy the represented object must be defiled or eliminated. The male becomes an object and inferior.

Once the course of action is decided, the Organized offender is calm and the internal conflict of stress is mostly eliminated... The offenders who get close and personal to their victim actually do not get emotionally involved. This dissociation maintains distance. Thus, they feel comfortable in the situations they are able to control.

There is no remorse or contrition. Everything is a matter of fact. They know the difference between right and wrong. <u>Changing wrong to right changes the standards.</u>

<u>This makes the consequences non-consequential.</u>

[1] Jung, CG, gen. ed., *Man and his Symbols*, 1964, p. 191964, p. 193.

[2] Douglas, John with Olshaker, Mark, *The Anatomy of Motive*, Pocket, 1999, p.9.

[3] Maslow, Abraham H., "A Theory of Human Motivation," *Psychological Review*, 1943, Vol. 50, No.4, pp. 370-396.

[4] Maslow, Abraham H., *Religions, Values and Peak Experiences*, Ohio State University Press, 1964.

[5] Estes, Clarissa Pinkola, *Women Who Run With Wolves: Myths and Stories of the Wild Woman Archetype*, Ballantine, (Psychology, Women's Studies), 1995, p. 11.

[6] Snyder, C. R.; Lopez, Shane J., (2007). *Positive Psychology*, Sage Publications, Inc., p. 147.

[7] Carlson, Neil R,; Heth C. Donald, (2007). *Psychology – the science of behavior*, Pearson Education, Canada, p. 700.

[8] deMause, Lloyd, *The History of Childhood*, Jason Aronson, 1995, pp. 51-54.

[9] deMause, Lloyd, *The Emotional Life of Nations*. Other Press, 2002.

[10] Knight, Chris, *Blood Relations: Menstruation and the Origins of Culture*, Yale University Press, 1991, pp. 22 and 432.

[11] Rubin, Harriet *The Princessa: Machiavelli for Women*, Doubleday, 1997, pp. 5, 8-9.

[12] Miller, Alice, trans. Hildegarde and Hunter Hannum, *For Your Own Good: Hidden Cruelty in child-rearing and the roots of violence*, Noonday Press – Farrar, Straus, Giroux, 1990, pp. 3-91.

[13] Ray, John J., "Punitive Personality Disorder," *The Journal of Social Psychology*, 1985, 125(3), 329-333.

[14] *National Institute of Mental Health*, 16 March 2016.

[15] Linehan, Marsha M., *Cognitive-behavioral treatment of borderline personality disorder*, Guilford Press, 1993, p. 146.

[16] Leichsenring, F.; Leibing, E., Kruse, J., New, A. S.; Leweke, F., (2011). "Borderline personality disorder," *The Lancet*, (9759): 74-84.

[17] Solomon, Robert C., University of Texas, Austin, *The Big Questions: A Short Introduction to Philosophy*, Harcourt Brace College Publishers, 1997, p. 326.

[18] Matteoli, Richard L., *Comixio Religious: The Socialization of Violence and Abuse*, Nemean Press, 2008. (A Mandated Report to Law Enforcement).

[19] Edinger, Edward, *Ego and Archetype: Individuation and the Religious Function of the Psyche*, Shambala, 1992, pp.3.

[20] Sigmund Freud, *On Metapsychology*, (PFL 11), p. 36.

[21] Gifis, Steven H., *Law Dictionary*, Barron's Educational Series, Inc.,1984, p. 55.

[22] Matteoli, Richard L., *Comixio Religious: The Socialization of Violence and Abuse*, Nemean Press, 2008. (A Mandated Report to Law Enforcement).

[23] Thomas, WI, "The Relation of the Medicine-Man to the Origin of the Professional Occupations," *Decennial Publications of the University of Chicago*, First Series, 4(1903): 241-256.

[24] Michaud, Stephen with Hazelwood, Roy, *The Evil That Men Do*, St. Martin's, 1998, p. 81-98.

[25] Baker, Caroline, *Reclaiming the Dark Feminine: The Price of Desire*, New Falcon, 1996, pp. 25-27.

[26] Editor, *Glen A. Costie (Veterans Affairs)*, Senior Executive Association: The professional association for career federal executives, ACTION Newsletter.

[27] Estes, Clarissa Pinkola, *Women Who Run With Wolves: Myths and Stories of the Wild Woman Archetype*, Ballantine, (Psychology, Women's Studies), 1995, pp. 8-11.

[28] Horrigan, Bonnie, *Red Moon Passage: The Power and Wisdom of Menopause*, Three Rivers Press, 1996, pp. 1-35.

[29] Graves, Robert, *The Greek Myths*, Penguin, 1992, p. 119. Origins of human sacrifice.

[30] Knight, Chris, *Blood Relations: Menstruation and the Origins of Culture*, Yale University Press, 1991, pp. iv and 42.

[31] Bennett, Jonah, "Leaked Tape: Union Prez Calls VA Chair 'A Fool,' Says He'll 'Whoop' VA Sec's 'Ass.' *The Daily Caller*, 02/11/2016.

[32] Meyers. Carol, *Discovering Eve*, Oxford University Press, 1988, p. 30.

[33] Editor, "American Federation of Government Employees Re-Elects National Officers," *PRNewswire AFGE*, August 18, 2015.

[34] Neumann, Erich, *The Great Mother*, Princeton University Press, 1991, pp. 211-225, 320-331. Transformation Mysteries: pp. 55-56 and 61-67.

[35] Eliade, Mircea, trans. Philip Mariet, *Images and Symbols: Studies in Religious Symbolism*, Princeton University Press, 1991, p. 39. The Great Round, the feminine representation, becomes the Sacred Center.

[36] Matteoli, Richard L., *Comixio Religious: The Socialization of Violence and Abuse*, Nemean Press, 2008. (A Mandated Report to Law Enforcement).

[37] Firestone, Shulamith, *The Dialectic of Sex: The Case for Feminine Revolution*, William Morrow and Company, 1970, pp, 1-2 and 41.

[38] Meyers. Carol, *Discovering Eve*, Oxford University Press, 1988, p. 41-42.

[39] Knight, Chris, *Blood Relations: Menstruation and the Origins of Culture*, Yale University Press, 1991, pp. 395, 270, 380, 385 and 432.

[40] Editor Fox News Politics, "Report: Retaliation by supervisors common at VA," *Associated Press*, July 21, 2014.

[41] Jeri-Jo Idarius, editor, "The Colors of My Heart: Giving a New Voice to Navaho Tradition: Interview with Sharon Burch," *Grace Millennium: Voices of Northern California Women*, Winter, 2001, pp. 52-57.

[42] Edinger, Edward, *TheMystery of THE CONIUNCTIO Alchemical Image of Indivuation*, Inner Cities Books: Studies in Jungian Psychology by Jungian Analysis, 1994.

[43] Douglas, John with Olshaker, Mark, *Mind Hunter: Inside the FBI's Elite Serial Crime Unit*, Pocket, 1995, p. 173.

[44] VAOIG, *Review of Alleged Data Manipulation at the VA Regional Office Houston, TX*, Department of Veterans Affairs, September 30, 2014.

[45] CNN Wire Staff, *Prudential considers changing payment of death benefits*, CNN, July 30, 2010.

[46] Bell, Catherine, *Ritual Theory, Ritual Practice*, Oxford University Press, 1992, pp. 23, 26, 54.

[47] House Committee on Veterans Affairs, *Esquire Executive-in-Charge and Vice Chairman, Board of Veterans Appeals, U.S, Department of Veterans Appeals*, Hearing on 01/22/2015: Veterans' Dilemma: Navigating the Appeals System for Veterans Claims.

[48] McElhatton, "Despite lie about degree, VA exec still overseas network of health care centers," *The Washington Times*, Monday, May 26, 2014.

[49] Bennett, Jonah, "Daily Caller: VA Secretary Robert McDonald Admits 'We Have A Leadership Crisis', *Daily Caller*, Oct. 8, 2015, Newsletter of Hon. Tim Huelskamp, Kansas.

[50] Matteoli, Richard L., *Comixio Religious: The Socialization of Violence and Abuse*, Nemean Press, 2008. (A Mandated Report to Law Enforcement).

[51] Bell, Catherine, *Ritual Theory, Ritual Practice*, Oxford University Press, 1992, p. 173-174.

[52] Ho, Vivian, "Oakland VA Office botched benefits, forgot about claims," *SFGate*, February 18, 2015.

[53] Eliade, Mircea, *The Myth of the Eternal Return*, Princeton University Press, 1954, p.3.

[54] Office of the Clerk, U.S. House of Representatives, U.S. Capitol, Room H- 154, Washington, Dc., 20515-6601, *Hearing: "Philadelphia and Oakland: Systematic Failures and Mismanagement"*, Committee on Veterans Affairs, Wednesday, April 22, 2015 (10:30 AM).

[55] De River, J. Paul and King, Brian, *The Sexual Criminal: A Psychoanalytical Study*, Bloat, 2000, p. 185.

[56] *Skipper.*

[57] Douglas, John with Olshaker, Mark, *Obsession*, Pocket, 1998, pp. 33-34.

[58] Bell, Catherine, *Ritual Theory, Ritual Practice*, Oxford University Press, 1992, p. 121.

[59] Garnier, J., *The Worship Of The Dead Or The Origins And Nature Of Pagan Idolatry And Its Bearing Upon The Early History Of Egypt and Babylonia*, Kessenger Publishing, 2006.

[60] Douglas, John with Olshaker, Mark, *Obsession*, Pocket, 1998, pp. 109-112 and 124.

[61] De River, J. Paul and King, Brian, *The Sexual Criminal: A Psychoanalytical Study*, Bloat, 2000, p. 188.

[62] Edwards, John Bel, Governor Louisiana, *Former Louisiana Department of Veterans Affairs Nurse Arrested on Felony Warrant*, State of Louisiana; Office of the Governor, Office of Inspector General, May 16, 2016.

[63] Burke, *The Exorcist.*

[64] Rosiak, Luke, "Union Officials Admit They Let Veterans Die Rather Than Talk To Republicans," *The Daily Caller*, 03/10/2016.

[65] J. R. Ewing, *Dallas.*

[66] Pleasance, Chris, "Bookkeeper accused of embezzling $830,000 from veterans' charity – using credit cards for lavish vacations and internet shopping," *Daily Mail*, 3 June 2014.

[67] Douglas, John with Olshaker, Mark, *Obsession*, Pocket, 1998, p. 352.

[68] Pawlyk, Oriana, "Report: VA IG ousted over indecent acts," *Military Times*, December 7, 2015.

[69] Yale Law School, Lillian Goldman Law Library, *Nuremburg Trial Proceedings*, Volume 4, Twenty-Fifth Day, Wednesday, 2, January 1946, Morning Session.

[70] U.S. Department of Health & Human Services, *Summary of the HIPPA Privacy Rules.*

[71] Douglas, John with Olshaker, Mark, *Journey into Darkness*, Pocket, 1995, pp. 22-34, 43, 66 and 75.

[72] Douglas, John with Olshaker, Mark, *The Anatomy of Motive*, Pocket, 1999, pp. 279, 262, 289-313, and 367.

GASLIGHTING

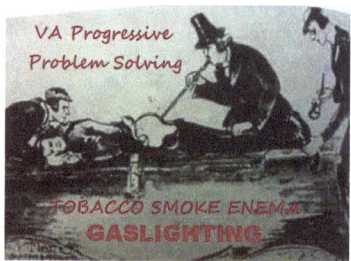

Gaslighting or gas-lighting is a form of mental abuse in which information is twisted or spun, selectively omitted to favor the abuser, or false information is presented with the intent of making victims doubt their own memory, perception, and sanity.

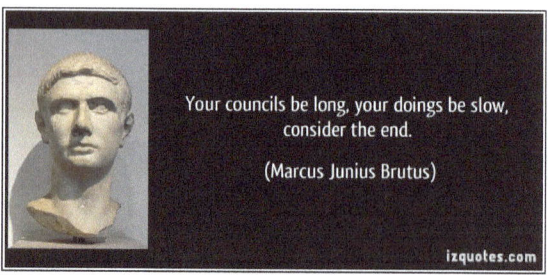

The Roadshow for Therapists
Working with Narcissistic Victim Abuse

The Effects of Gaslighting in Narcissistic Victim Syndrome

What is "Gaslighting"?

Gaslighting is a form of psychological abuse used by narcissists in order to instill in their victim's an extreme sense of anxiety and confusion to the point where they no longer trust their own memory, perception or judgment. The techniques used in "Gaslighting" by the narcissist are similar to those used in brainwashing, interrogation, and torture that have been used in psychological warfare by intelligence operative, law enforcement and other forces for decades.

The intention is to, in a systematic way, target the victim's mental equilibrium, self confidence, and self esteem so that they are no longer able to function in an independent way. Gaslighting involves the abuser to frequently and systematically withhold factual information from the victim, and replacing it with false information. Because of it's subtly, this cunning Machiavellian behaviour is a deeply insidious set of manipulations that is difficult for anybody to work out, and with time it finally undermines the mental stability of the victim. That is why it is such a dangerous form of abuse. The emotional damage of Gaslighting is huge on the narcissistic victim. When they are exposed to it for long enough, they begin to lose their sense of their own self. Unable to trust their own judgments, they start to question the reality of everything in their life. They begin to find themselves second-guessing themselves, and this makes them become very insecure around their decision making, even around the smallest of choices. The victim becomes depressed and withdrawn, they become totally dependent on the abuser for their sense of reality. In effect the gaslighting 'turns the victim's reality on its head.

Where does the term "Gaslighting" come from?

The term "Gaslighting" comes from the 1944 Hollywood classic movie called Gaslight. The film starts with the murder of the famous opera singer Alice Alquist in London. The perpetrator was after the stars jewels, but before he could get them, he was interrupted by her young niece Paula (played by Ingrid Bergman); a child that Alice had reared after the death of her own mother. To help her get over the trauma of Alice's death, Paula is sent to live in Italy, where she studies opera with her aunty Alice's old teacher for several years. While in Italy, she meets a charismatic older man named Gregory Anton (played by Charles Boyer), they have a whirl-wind romance and very soon she marries him. He persuades her that they should return to London to live in the house bequeathed to her by her aunt. When they arrive, hidden in a book, Paula finds a letter addressed to her aunt Alice, it was from a man called Sergius Bauer. The letter was dated two days before the murder. Gregory reacts violently to the letter, but recovers his composure quickly, and justifies his outburst as vexation at seeing his lovely bride relive bad memories. Once Alice's things are removed into the attic, Gregory's diabolical psychopathic behaviour becomes very bizarre indeed. Almost immediately he sets out, systematically and methodically, to deliberately drive Paula insane by psychologically manipulating their environment covertly; for example, when a picture is missing from the wall, Gregory tells her that she took it, but Paula cannot recall having done so.

Secretly, Gregory gains entry into the attic and begins to tamper with the gas-light there, causing the rest of the lamps in the house to become dim. When Paula mentions hearing footsteps coming from the attic, and seeing the lights dimming for no apparent reason, he tells her it's all in her imagination, and that he does not see any change in the brightness of the lights. He does not stop there, he resorts to other means of deception to further confuse his wife. For example, he fires his wife's trusted elderly maid, replacing her with a younger one (Nancy) that he can seductively control. When Paula complains of feeling hurt and humiliated by his behaviour with Nancy, he tell her he is only being friendly. He states that in Europe no woman would feel humiliated for such a trivial act. Convinced that the wife is insane, Nancy begins to treat her with contempt, and Paula can feel her loathing, which further distresses her. He then takes command of all outside influences so that he has complete control over Paula, making it easier to manipulate her sense of reality. Of course, he pretends to have genuine concern for Paula, but the bottom-line is that he is only concerned about isolating her. Having isolated her from those within the house, he then precedes to take command of all outside influences so that he has complete control over her. He stops all visitors, and he does not allow her to leave the house. He implies that he is doing this for her own good, because her "kleptomania and imaginings" are due to her nervous disposition. On the rare occasion when they do go to a gathering at a friend's house, he shows her his watch chain, from which his watch was missing. When he searches her handbag he mysteriously finds it there. Horrified, she becomes so hysterical that Gregory has to take her home immediately. She is convinced that there is something very wrong with her, and that it is best that she no longer goes out in public. Gregory's overall goal is to drive Paula out of her mind so that she can have her certified insane and institutionalized. He continually tells her that she is ill and fragile, until confused and scared, Paula begins to act more erratically, and she starts to internalize that she is becoming the fragile person that he says she is. He even begins to rearrange items in the house, and then he accuses her of "always losing things". Cruelly, he tells her that she is losing her memory. Knowing that her mother had died insane, to demoralize her further by viciously convincing her that she has inherited her mother's bad genes. The more she doubts herself, the more desperate she is for her husband's approval and love, but he rejects her, insisting that she is insane. With a combination of seduction, deception, isolation, bullying and rejection, reluctantly Paula starts to accept that she is losing her mind, and she becomes totally dependent on him for her sense of reality.

Unbeknown to Paula, Gregory is not who she thinks he is, little does she know that in fact he is her aunt's murderer, Sergius Bauer. It was no coincidence that he happened upon her in Italy. He had deliberately gone to search her out with the intention of seducing her into

---

Recognizing Narcissistic Traits Before It Is Too Late

Revealing the Two faces of Narcissism: Overt and Covert

The Effects of Gaslighting in Narcissistic Victim Syndrome

THE NARCISSISTIC EPIDEMIC ... The "Me First" Culture

The Narcissists Addiction to Adrenaline

The Narcissists Addiction to Fame

The Narcissists Addiction to Grandiosity

The place of "Cognitive Dissonance" in Narcissistic Victim Syndrome

The Place of Myths In the Understanding of Narcissistic Personality Disorder

The Typical Narcissistic Woman As A Friend

Understanding Narcissistic Injury

Understanding the phenomenon of Narcissistic Supply

Was Raoul Moat a narcissist?

What Causes Narcissists To Rage?

WHAT DOES THE BIBLE SAY ABOUT NARCISSISTIC BEHAVIOUR?

What Exactly is Narcissism? (Explaining the Many Facets of Narcissism)

What is Infantile Regression?

What is Stockholm Syndrome?

marrying him. His main objective was to gain entry into the house in London where he could continue his search for Alice's jewels. It was his rummaging in the attic for the jewels that Paula had heard, and it was he that had caused the flickering of the lights (from the attic) when he reduced the flow of gas to the downstairs lights. She had become an impediment to his search, so he needed her certified insane and institutionalized so that he could be free to find his treasure. He came very near to realizing his goal, but by some chance encounter Paula meets Inspector Brian Cameron of Scotland Yard (acted by Joseph Cotten), who was an avid admirer of her Aunt Alice. He tells her that she is not going out of her mind, but that she is beings slowly and systematically been driven out of your mind by her husband. Together with Paula, and with the support of the old housekeeper (who had suspected the master of causing these events), he opens the "cold case". The drama reaches its final conclusion when he arrests Gregory just as he has found his treasure of the long lost jewels.

What is the purpose of "gaslightings"?

As you can see, this "Gaslighting Tango" is a form of psychological warfare that is both deliberate and progressive in nature between one individual (the gaslighter) and another (the gaslightee). The Gaslighting Effect involves an insidious set of psychological manipulations that are carried out gradually in stages, and repeated time after time, in order to undermine the mental stability of its victim. It is truly a convoluted dance, where finally the unsuspecting gaslightee believes that they are going crazy. Anyone can become the victim of these gaslighting maneuvers; age, intelligence, gender, creed is no barrier against narcissistic abuse of this kind. It does not only happen in romantic relationships (such as Paula & Gregory above), it can occur in all different types of relationships: between parent and child, siblings, friends, and work colleague. Actually, it can happen between any two people in any walk of life if the intention is there. The gaslighting, as a harassment technique, starts with a series of subtle mind games that intentionally prays on the gaslightee's limited ability to tolerate ambiguity or uncertainty. This is done in order to undercut the victim's trust in their own sense of reality and sense of self, thus resulting in confusion and perplexity for the victim. Even when the victim is bewildered and left wondering, "What just happened there?", there is a reluctance to see the gaslighter for what they are, actually it is this denial that is the cornerstone of the gaslighting relationship.

The "Puppet Master's" Web of Deceit:

Narcissists are puppet masters who manipulate their victims for personal gain. With precision they are able to "pull the strings" of their victims without detection, and render them helpless. In order to understand how a person can become a victim of a narcissist in the first place, it is important to know that the narcissist has many faces (the proverbial man or woman for all seasons). Different faces are required by the abuser as they lead the relationship through different phases; The Idealization Stage, Devaluation Stage, and the Discard Stage. The good news is that the gaslighting does not happen all at once, it happens in stages, which means that if one suspects (in the early stages) that they are being gaslighted, they can protect themselves by walking away (physically or metaphorically). However, one needs to be informed as to what those stages look like, in that way, the individual will be able to understand and identify what is happening at these different stages. With this information, one will be able to spot if they are being gaslighted in any interpersonal-relationship (whether it is at home, work or socially), and guard themselves by keeping the narcissist out of their energy field.

Gaslighing techniques (3 Stages):

The Idealization Stage:

During the initial "idealization stage", the narcissist puts on their "best face" in order to mould their victim into a symbiotic relationship with them as their narcissistic supply. In the beginning of the relationship the narcissist showers the victim with attention, they are loving, charming, flirtatious, energetic, exciting, and great fun to be with. They appear to be so happy and interested in the relationship, and the unsuspecting victim enjoys every moment with their new charismatic partner. They love how the narcissist is so beautifully intense and how they get drunk on life, and they too want to drink this elixir with them. Intense bonding begins for the victim, and innocently, they also believe that the partner feels the same way about them, that the relationship is reciprocal, but this is the narcissist's biggest deception. Caught up in this alluring state of euphoria, the victim becomes "hooked" by the gaslighter's exuberance and grandiose exaggerations. In this kind of relationship, victims are known to experience biochemical changes in the body and structural changes in the brain. These exciting hooks create a release of chemicals (endorphins) in the brain, and it is these endorphins (or pleasure substances) that make the victim feel the euphoria in the first phase of the relationship. Like any addict, they become addicted to that high, and very soon they find themselves hooked emotionally to their narcissistic suitor too. However, this honeymoon phase is only an illusion, all smoke and mirrors. Having expertly determined the victim's strengths and weaknesses, the "Idealization Phase" is over, and it is time for the devaluation stage of the gaslighting to begin. From here on in, the narcissist seems to turn cold, unfeeling, and even bitingly cruel.

The Devaluation Stage:

The relationship has now shifted into the "devaluation phase", and it is as if a lethal freak fog has descended over the relationship. Almost overnight the narcissist becomes decisively cold and uncaring. The victim's falls from grace is a hard one, they cannot seem to do anything right anymore; the narcissists loving words turn to criticism, everything the victim tries ends in a negative effect, and they find themselves devalued at every turn. Totally confused, the victim has no idea what is happening, and they become increasingly stressed, unhappy and depressed with the situation. The roller-coaster relationship leaves the victim in a state of constant chaos, as if always "walking on eggshells". All their energy is directed at defending themselves, so the narcissist is not getting the positive attention that they crave; this is likely to be the time when the narcissist starts to look for a fresh provider of narcissistic supply.

The narcissist gaslighting is now at its peak, and there is no reasoning with them. Confused by the narcissist's bizarre behaviour, the victim works harder and harder to please their abuser in the hopes of getting the relationship back to where it was in the start, when it felt safe. Deprived of their "narcissistic drug", the victim is suddenly thrown into strong withdrawal symptoms. They are distraught with anxiety, turned inside out with confusion, and bereft of what they though they had, a soul-mate. In order to cope with the pain of this deep wound of abandonment and rejection, they escape into a range of unconscious defense mechanisms (a mix of denial, rationalization, infantile regressive patterns, cognitive dissonance, trauma bonding etc.). Alone and isolated from the real world, these behaviours becomes their only way of surviving the narcissistic abuse, and the gaslighting they are now experiencing. No matter what they do, they only seem to create narcissistic injury to this stranger; and each time they do that, they inadvertently release an almighty rage down upon themselves (without even knowing how they are doing it). By merely engaging in these survival tactics, the victim becomes the hostage that is overly dependent on their captive (Stockholm Syndrome), where unpredictability and uncertainty is the order of their day. As a result, they are now caught in the macabre dance with the narcissist's pathological grandiose self, where hell reigns supreme, and they regress into infantile regressive patterns of behaviour (Regressed Infantilism). At this stage they are most likely suffering the effects of Narcissistic Victim Syndrome (NVS), where they are reduced to a shadow of their former self. Finally they are at the mercy of the whims and pleasures of their "puppet master".

The narcissist despises who their supply person has become; they view them as powerless, inferior and worthless victims, but at the same time, their worthless prey is providing them with a bountiful amount of narcissistic supply. Therein lays the paradox; the more the victim shows their distress, the more they become narcissistic supply for the abuser, and the more important and powerful the abuser gets to feel. The more important and powerful the abuser feels, the more blatant their verbal and physical violent becomes. This "pull-push" scenario leaves the narcissist acting in a way that says, "I hate you, but don't you dare leave me or I will kill you". They will react to any perceived movement away from them as a threat to their narcissistic supply, therefore any show of self-determination by the victim will surly be devalued. The narcissist is merciless in the way they devalue the victim. Devaluation of the victim can be delivered through many different forms and levels of attack; through victims own attachment needs, their intellectual capabilities, physical body, sexuality, creativity etc. By this time, like Pavlov's dogs, the victim has been conditioned, and appears to the outside world that they are willing partners in the narcissists "convoluted dance". Even if they do manage to escape from that narcissistic individual, they are at high risk of future re-victimization and entrapment with other narcissists, because they are primed in a way that other narcissists can spot.

The Discarding Phase:

In this phase, the game comes to its final conclusion. What started out as the idealization of a victim by the narcissist, is doomed to end with the idealization of the narcissist by the victim's over dependence. Once this happens, the narcissist ardor for the game has dampened, in their eyes they have already won the contest, and the fun is over. By this time, the narcissist is totally indifferent to any needs or wishes that the victim may have, in effect they no longer exist in their mind. Not so for the victim, they are left confused and raw with emotion, and are eager to find solutions in order to "fix" the dying relationship. However, the narcissist resists all attempts to rescue the relationship, they will bully with silence, or if there is any kind of response, it will be brutally cold. In effect, the victim has become "worthlessly inferior" to them; they know they have drained the victim dry, that they have now outlived their usefulness, and now it is time for the narcissist to move on to the next source of supply. Any undertaking to win them back by the victim will only feed the narcissists ego, and further provide them with a transient source of narcissistic supply.

The plight of the victims of the Gaslighting Effect:

During the process of gaslighting, the victim will find themselves going through emotional and psychological states of mind. In her wonderful book, The Gaslighting Effect, Robin Stern, Ph.D. speaks of three stages the victim will go through: Disbelief, Defense, and Depression, she also goes on to flags down warning signs for recognizing when one is being gaslighted. I would like to expand a little on her analysis.

Disbelief:

Gaslighting is an extreme form of emotional abuse used by the narcissistic gaslighter to manipulate the innocent victim (gaslightee). The effects of gaslighting are so insidious, that they can lead to the victim losing all trust in their own judgment and reality. The victim's initial reaction to the gaslighting behaviour is one of utter disbelief; they cannot believe the sudden change towards them, or indeed the fact that they are being gaslighted in the first place. All they know is that something terribly odd seems to be happening in the relationship, but they cannot figure out what it is that is happening. Of course, this is precisely what the abuser wants, after all, it would not work if the victim knew what was happening. The methods used by the narcissist in the initial idealization stage of the relationship progresses in such a way that it virtually guarantees that the victim will become hooked utterly and completely to their narcissistic abuser. Blinded by their love after been totally seduced, the victim naturally, trusts genuinely that their love is reciprocated, but of course, this is untrue, a total fabrication. Where once the abuser's communication with the victim had been accessible and stayed within the relationship, it has now become blocking and diverting. All they know is that where the narcissist had once held them in "good heart", they have now become highly critical of them. The sympathy and support that had been available has now turned to distain and antagonism. Whenever the victim (gaslightee) wants to reasonably discuss what is happening in the relationship, they are meet with silence, or worse, they find that everything that is being said is twisted or trivialized.

It is important to realize that the gaslighting does not need to be severe in order to have severe consequences on the victim, it can be as subtle as being told that "you are so sensitive", or that they should not do something because "you are not able to do it, leave it to me". Even though the victim can rationalize that these statements are untrue, gradually their confidence is being eroded away to such an extent that they cannot trust themselves. Gaslighting strokes, such as moving items from place to place, and then the abuser denying that they had moved the item really creates huge confussion to the victim. Or saying something, then later denying that they had said such a thing. All of this psychological warfare has the effect of making the victim doubt their own memory or perception of events. Desperate for the gaslighter's approval and reassurance that they are not going mad, the victim becomes very dependent on their narcissistic abuser for a sense of reality.

Defense:

At this stage the victim still has enough of their self to fight and defend themselves against the gaslighting manipulation. However, the narcissist's "gaslighting" is beginning to do what it is intended to do, that is, to throw the victim off balance by creating self-doubt, angst, turmoil, and guilt. This emotional damage causes the victim, over time, to lose their sense of reality, and sense of self. Becoming lost, confused, and unable to trust their own instincts and memory, they tend to isolate themselves somewhat because of the shame they feel. Before long their psychic energy becomes depleted, and they are left unable to defend themselves from the horrendous gaslighting effect. At this stage the person's whole system may feel that it is in danger of annihilation.

From birth, nature builds in unconscious defense mechanisms and adaptive behaviours in order to protect the child from annihilation from early trauma, and these same defenses remain throughout life when ever we are vulnerable to highly stressful experiences that threaten us with annihilation. When the child starts life, they experience the world as a frightening place, so in order to reduce their fear they need to form an emotional bond with somebody in order to reduce their stress and anxiety. They identify and bond with their main caregiver (usually the Mother), and of course, they are very likely, at some time in the future, to experience her as their first aggressor. Mother can be experienced by the child as being both "threatening and kind", and this seems to lead to the child turning to emotional bonding for survival. This psychological condition is known to-day as "Stockholm Syndrome". It is found to happen universally in situations where people find themselves to be held captive and in fear of their lives; as in kidnapping, hostage situations, and narcissistic abuse. This phenomenon of trauma bonding with the narcissist aggressor can be found in Narcissistic Victim Syndrome. In Stockholm Syndrome, the victim adapts to the traumatic situation by unconsciously going into an regressive mode, where they return to childish infantile patterns of behaviour (Regressed Infantilism), and bond with their captor as they did with their mother earlier in life as a defense against annihilation. In order to cope with the discomfort of living within such madness, the victims motivational drive provides a way that they can rationalize to reduce the dissonance they are experiencing (Cognitive Dissonance). For the therapist to understand the dynamics of all these defense mechanisms, they will then be able to appreciate why victims stay in these narcissistic abusive relationships, as it is a clever, but complicated unconscious self survival strategy.

Depression:

By this stage the victim can hardly recognize themselves, they are quickly becoming a shadow of their former self. Living under tyranny within a war zone where they are controlled, physically and emotionally battered, unable to make decisions, subjected to constant rages, sucked dry, stripped of dignity and safety, they exist in a joyless life. They begin to feel that they can't do anything right any more, they don't feel that they can trust their own mind, and they withdraw with a skewed reality of what is really taking place. They escape into depression. Many victims will also go on to experience Post Traumatic Stress Disorder (PTSD). The diagnosis of PDSD can be made based on certain symptoms being present, and these symptoms fall into three categories:

1. Reliving: (Flashbacks, intrusive imagery, nightmares, anxiety etc)
2. Avoidance: (Avoiding people, places or thoughts, emotional numbing, lack of interest, hopelessness etc).

3. Arousal: (Difficulty concentrating, irritability, outbursts of anger, insomnia, hyper-vigilance etc).

In my work with Narcissistic Victim Syndrome I have noticed that the victims were brought to the place of annihilation and death on many levels of the self while experiencing gaslighting behaviour in their narcissistic relationships. When we take on the journey of recovery together, I take care and time to educate the individual as to what was happening to them as their story unfolds. I am always meet with an array of responses, from shock, disbelief, profound sadness, guilt, shame, anger, fear, reflection, loneliness and an array of physical symptoms (panic attacks, flashbacks, anxious negative thoughts, fatigue, eating disorders, dissociation, abreaction etc.), but they also express relief at finally knowing what had been going on in the relationship, and the amount of "losses" they were dealing with. I think many of the stages are very similar to Elisabeth Kübler-Ross stages of grief, which are Denial, Anger, Bargaining, Depression, and Acceptance. But still, I find that the individual holds the key to even more strategies for guarding the various levels of defense that I have mentioned here. I am always amazed at how surprisingly resilient these victims are. All our strategies for surviving are incredibly intelligent, and together (the client and I) welcome each and every one as a teacher for our learning and understanding. When this happens, it allows for all the fragmented parts of the soul to return home where they become like special guests at a glorious Banquet, one unifying whole sitting at the Table of Recovery. When a therapist experiences this work they will truly appreciate and understand the deep suffering these victims have gone through daily. The fact that these clients have survived the torturous effects of the disorganized narcissistic personality disorder is in itself a miracle, and a testament to the human spirit.

Robin Stern names some of the warning signs of the effects of Gaslighting, I am merely expanding on some of these below:

What are the warning signs of Gaslighting?

- **Second-guessing:** Because a victim has had their confidence eroded by the constant gaslighting, they live in fear of doing the wrong thing, and making their situation even more dangerous for themselves. They invariably find themselves asking "what if", and always trying to second guess themselves. This often effects how they problem-solve, and make decisions in their life.

- **Asking "Am I too sensitive?":** Projection and blame are the hallmarks of gaslighting, and the victim become hyper-sensitive to the constant humiliation of their abuser. They hear countless times that they are "too sensitive", that they soon begin to believe the lies. As a result they look for approval before doing anything, fearful that they will make more mistakes that will end in more humiliation. This form of gaslighting makes the victim doubt everything about themselves, so they constantly ask, "Am I being too sensitive".

- **Apologizing:** Living with the narcissistic Dr. Jekyll and Mr/s Hyde, the victim finds themselves always apologizing for "never doing things right", they even apologize for their very existence; it is a way of avoiding more conflict with their aggressor. Apology is not just something the victim does to be polite; it is a powerful strategy for staying safe while in the war zone, and a means to disarm the anger of the gaslighter. Most importantly, the power of apology is that it can take the shame off the narcissist and redirect it towards the victim, therefore avoiding some of the narcissists rage.

- **Lack joy and happiness in life (melancholy):** If one lives under the constant tyranny of the gaslighting narcissist, they can expect extremes of lethal hostility. Many victims go through physical and mental torture that can cause them to suffer a personality change, leaving them feeling confused, lonely, frightened and unhappy. Often they continue to carry this melancholy even after they escape from the abuser.

- **Withholding information from others:** Victims experience great shame about their situation; they get tired of trying to cover up their abuse as they go along. When well meaning friends and family members tell them they are being abused, they avoid the subject, and soon they learn to withhold giving more information in order to avoid further conflict. The importance of shame in narcissistic abuse is a difficult issue, but I don't think it is too difficult to accept that the crimes of the gaslighting narcissist stigmatize the victim to their very core. Their shame is a normal response to the social failure they so often feel as a result of their abuse (i.e. the shame of being unable to protect themselves from their abuse). This shame can be seen as defensiveness and withdrawal by others. The relationship between shame and social supports is too complex to deal with here.

• **Knowing something is terribly wrong, but can't figure out what:** The goal of gaslighting is to control and influence the reality of the gaslightee. It only works when the victim is unaware of what is really happening. The more the victim doubts their own reality or competence, the more dependent they become of the abuser. It is a vicious circle of events that is totally confusing to the victim, and that is exactly what the gaslighter wants.

• **Trouble making simple decisions:** To be caught in the narcissistic web of deception and illusion is the equivalent to being a fly trapped in the spider's web. When entering the web, does the victim know that it is about to be bound up and eaten alive any more than the fly? The answer is "no". However, the narcissistic web is akin to the disintegration of the self; the victim, under the threat of continual danger, forms a psychic bond with the abuser in order to avoid fragmentation of the self. In forming that bond they are compelled to organize themselves around their idealized abuser's desires, and surrender their authentic potential. Having to ask permission to do anything, not being aloud to have their own opinion, never allowed to win the argument, constantly being chastised and humiliated, compromising their own thoughts, values, needs, and belief. Understandably, caught in this web they lose all autonomy, even their ability to make decisions for their own self.

• **You have the sense that you used to be a very different person – more confident, more fun-loving, and more relaxed:** In order to survive, the victim enters into what is termed the "the narcissists dance". This is an unconscious defense mechanism which helps to keep the victim safe, but in so doing they almost lose themselves by placating, complying, and appeasing. This becomes part of their way of being, a great "pleaser" with everybody. Unless this unconscious dance is exposed in therapy, and the victim educated about narcissistic behavior, they are actually left vulnerable to becoming Narcissistic Supply yet again. The reason is that they are conditioned (like Pavlov's dogs) in a way that makes them a target for other hungry narcissists, who are always on the hunt for new supply, and are quick to spot those primed already.

• **You feel hopeless and joyless:** What had once seemed like heaven has now turned into a hell. There is no peace or joy in this place, just fear and suppression. Life loses all hope, as if the light has been turned off. All that remains is the deep black cloud of depression. And the victim is forced to live in a state of acquiescence in order to survive. Their perceptions of reality are continually undermined by the gaslighting sham, so they end up losing confidence in their intuition, memory, or reasoning powers. They are spun lies, lies that tell them that they are over-sensitive, imagining, unreasonable, irrational, over-reacting, and that they have no right to be upset. Hearing this time and time again, their reality is turned inside out, and they begin to believe that this may all be true.

The narcissist's form of psychological abuse has managed to instill in their victim an extreme sense of anxiety and confusion to the point where they no longer trust their own memory, perception or judgment. In this state they are truly a hostage. However, many manage to get the courage to break free, but this is usually after several painful attempts. But when they do finally escape, in time they may find their way to your therapy room. Your job is to not just do the recovery work with them, but also to educate them about the traits and effects of narcissistic abuse. That way you give them back their reality and power, and they will be in a position to be able to recognize the narcissist at work, and be equipt to guard themselves against further re-victimization. Don't underestimate the power of recovery of these people; the fact that they have survived such extreme abuse is testament to their strength and determination. I never fail to be amazed at the resilience of the human spirit.

MAGAZINE   COMPASSIONATE ACTIVISM   SPEAKERS   SEARCH   COURSE LOGIN

everyday feminism

FEM 101   PRIVILEGE   TRANS & GNC   RACE   LGBTQIA   CLASS   RELIGION   SEX   LOVE   BODY   DISABILITY   VIOLENCE   VIDEOS   COMICS

WHAT'S HOT RIGHT NOW

3 Ways My Parents Unintentionally Taught Me That My Consent Didn't Matter

5 Microaggressions Secular People Often Hear – And Why They're Wrong

Gaslighting Is a Common Victim-Blaming Abuse Tactic – Here Are 4 Ways to Recognize It in Your Life

4 Reasons Why We Need to Stop Thinking of Skinny-Shaming as 'Reverse Discrimination'

report this ad

10 Things I've Learned About Gaslighting As An Abuse Tactic

August 27, 2015 by Shea Emma Fett

f   ⌄   t   Total Shares 135.3K

FREE ARTICLES

Enter Your Email Here

CLICK TO SUBSCRIBE

Originally published on Medium and cross-posted here with their permission.

Gaslighting is the attempt of one person to overwrite another person's reality.

There's a good chance that you now know more about gaslighting than most therapists.

Source: iStock

And that is really unfortunate, because if you have experienced gaslighting, it's going to be really hard to untangle it yourself.

Unfortunately, you may have to, and I want to tell you that you are not alone.

Let me share my experience. Here are ten things I wish I'd known at the beginning. Let's do this together.

SEARCH FOR ARTICLES

Search the site ...

1. Gaslighting Doesn't Have to Be Deliberate

About the fifth time I called a close friend of mine on the phone, gasping for air, asking "Am I a monster?" he finally said, "Emma, he's gaslighting you."

53

Wikipedia told me that it came from an old movie, where the main character makes changes in the environment and then insists to his victim that she is simply imagining these changes.

Whaat? I thought. *My partner isn't doing that. I could not imagine him plotting and manipulating my environment or our interactions to make me feel crazy. He's a human being who is hurt, who I keep hurting. It's me, not him.*

Unfortunately, the first definition I looked up was woefully inadequate. Gaslighting does not require deliberate plotting. Gaslighting only requires a belief that it is acceptable to overwrite another person's reality.

The rest just happens organically when a person who holds that belief feels threatened. We learn how to control and manipulate each other very naturally.

The distinguishing feature between someone who gaslights and someone who doesn't is an internalized paradigm of ownership. And in my experience, identifying that paradigm is a lot easier than spotting the gaslighting.

Gaslighting tends to follow when intimidation is no longer acceptable.

I believe that gaslighting is happening culturally and interpersonally on an unprecedented scale, and that this is the result of a societal framework where we pretend everyone is equal while trying simultaneously to preserve inequality.

You can see it in the media constantly.

For instance, every time an obvious hate crime is portrayed as an isolated case of mental illness, this is gaslighting. The media is saying to you, *What you know to be true is not true.*

Intimate partner violence wasn't seen as a serious crime until the 1970s. So, did we, in the last forty years, address the beliefs that cause intimate partner violence? No.

But now if you abuse your partner, you're usually considered to be a bad person. So what do you do, with all the beliefs that would lead you to violence, if violence is no longer an acceptable option?

You use manipulation, and you use gaslighting.

2. Manipulation and Gaslighting Are Distinct Behaviors

Maybe a better way to put this is that gaslighting is a type of manipulation, but not the only type.

Manipulation usually centers around a direct or indirect threat that is made in order to influence another person's behavior. Gaslighting uses threats as well, but has the goal of actually changing who someone is, not just their behavior.

It's important to recognize that gaslighting and garden variety manipulation are not the same.

Both will degrade your self-esteem, but gaslighting, when effective, will actually damage your trust in yourself and your experience of reality.

FOLLOW US ON FACEBOOK

ADVERTISEMENTS

MOST POPULAR THIS MONTH

3 Ways My Parents Unintentionally Taught Me That My Consent Didn't Matter

8 Signs Your Yoga Practice Is Culturally Appropriated – And Why It Matters

3. Gaslighting Doesn't Always Involve Anger or Intimidation

The book *The Gaslight Effect* refers to a type of gaslighting called glamor gaslighting.

This is where the gaslighter showers you with special attention, but never actually gives you what you need. They put you on a pedestal, but then they're not there. In fact, *they may get angry at you* when you need a shoulder to cry on.

It becomes difficult, after a while, to identify why it is that you feel so alone and hollow.

In another type of gaslighting, the gaslighter is always transformed into the victim. Whenever you bring up a problem, you find yourself apologizing by the end of the conversation.

For me, these were the worst exchanges.

Every gaslighter/gaslightee relationship is different, but for me, there was a very specific pattern. I would say something to him. He would have a very strong emotional reaction to it, far above what I would have anticipated. I would backtrack to try figure out what I had said and how to make it better.

He would accuse me of inconsistency when I backtracked.

I would try to explain that I was adjusting to try to communicate best with him, because clearly I was failing.

He would tell me that my inconsistency implied that I was lying.

I would say, "No, no, I know I'm not lying. Maybe I just can't remember it right."

"It seems I can't trust your memory," he would say.

We would never return to the original issue. I usually ended up crying hysterically.

4. It's Normal Not to Be Able to Remember What Happened

This, more than anything, is something I wish I had known.

It was a secret I kept, that fed my self doubt and guilt for years after I left. I used to black out. I remember conversations where I would start standing in the kitchen and end up in a ball on the floor.

Just days after it happened, I wouldn't be able to remember what happened in the time in between. I wouldn't even be able to remember what the conversation was about. My abuser accused me of abuse while I was with him – and then publicly for years after.

It's one of the reasons I left – because I couldn't figure out what I was doing or how to fix it, and I couldn't bear the thought that I might be abusive to someone. I've ripped my memories apart, trying to figure what it was that he experienced. What it was that I did.

And I have found some things in me that needed to change, as all people who look deeply at their abusive tendencies will find. But I couldn't, in my own memory, find what it was that he saw in me.

10 Ways Your Social Justice Work Mig Be Inaccessible and Elitist (And Why That's a Problem)

6 Signs Your Call-Out Isn't Actually About Accountability

ADVERTISEMENTS

report this ad

report this ad

MOST POPULAR THIS WEEK

3 Ways My Parents Unintentionally Taught Me That My Consent Didn't Matter

I could not find the narcissist. I could not find the vicious manipulator. I could not find the home wrecker. But I had black spots in my memory. Completely black. And I wondered, *is that when it happened? Is that when I abused him?*

Losing spots in your memory makes it very plausible when someone tells you that they cannot trust your memory. It makes it very plausible when they tell you that you are abusive.

But it's normal to lose your memory when you're being gaslighted. In fact, it is one of the signs that you should look for. It's a good sign that it might be time to leave.

Why Saying 'It's My Choice' Doesn't Necessarily Make Your Choice Femini

5. There Are Distinct Stages (And These Stages Can Progress After the Relationship Is Over)

A gaslighter doesn't simply need to be right. They also need for *you* to believe that they are right.

In stage one, you know that they're being ridiculous, but you argue anyways.

You argue for hours, without resolution. You argue over things that shouldn't be up for debate – your feelings, your opinions, your experience of the world.

You argue because you need to be right, you need to be understood, or you need to get their approval.

In stage one, you still believe yourself, but you also unwittingly put that belief up for debate.

In stage two, you consider your gaslighter's point of view first and try desperately to get them to see your point of view as well.

You continue to engage because you're afraid of what their perspective of you says about you.

Winning the argument now has one objective: proving that you're still good, kind, and worthwhile.

In stage three, when you're hurt, you first ask, "What's wrong with me?"

You consider their point of view as normal. You start to lose your ability to make your own judgements. You become consumed with understanding them and seeing their perspective. You live with and obsess over every criticism, trying to solve it.

Looking back, I see that I was deep in stage two when I left the relationship. However, I continued to try to have a friendship with him for months after. I longed for resolution, understanding, and forgiveness.

And when I finally went no contact, instead of healing, *I actually moved into stage three.* I didn't understand, nor did I know how to solve, the gaslighting that I continued to do to myself after the relationship was over.

If I could go back and give myself one piece of advice, it'd be to go *no contact* immediately for at least a year. And maybe that's what other might need, too.

It's really, really hard. It's hard because it may still feel like that understanding and resolution is right around the corner. It's hard to let go of that.

But think: You don't have to vote. Just commit to a week. Because anyone who isn't abusive won't punish you for the space you need to heal.

And when I say "no contact," I mean complete no contact. Distance yourself from mutual friends. Block your gaslighter on social media. Ask your friends not to give you any new information about them unless it directly pertains to your safety.

Fuck anyone who says you are being unreasonable.

You need this to heal, and you need the space to learn how to stop gaslighting yourself.

6. There Are Distinct Traits That Make You More Susceptible to Gaslighting, But They Can Also Be Super Powers

There are three tendencies that will pull you into a gaslighting exchange. These tendencies are the need to be right, the need to be understood, and the need for approval.

Additionally, certain traits – such as being empathic, being a caretaker, needing to see your partner in a positive light, and being a "people pleaser" – might make you more susceptible.

But I would strongly urge you to not go in and try to crush these wonderful things about you.

You care strongly about your ideas, and about other people. You want to understand and be understood. You care about your effect on other people, and you're willing to change to accommodate the people around you.

And ironically, your gaslighter probably told you that you were selfish and cruel and oblivious. And then perhaps your therapist told you that you need to stop caring so much because it draws you into abuse. What to do?

Empathy is important. It's important for all of us. It makes me angry when people tell me that my empathy is a weakness. My empathy is a super power. My desire and ability to empathize kept me locked into a cycle of abuse, yes. But my desire to empathize wasn't the problem.

The ability to hear criticism and then to change yourself for the better based on that feedback is also a fucking super power. Don't let anyone tell you otherwise. My problem was not my willingness to change, but my willingness to change for the wrong reasons.

Change should make you bigger. It should increase your tank of self-love. It should make you stronger, clearer, more directed, more differentiated, and more compassionate.

The pain of growth is different than the pain of destruction. One will fill you with love and pride, even when it's hard, and the other will fill you with shame and fear.

No one should use shame or fear to try to get you to change. When they do this, they're not asking for change – they're asking for control.

7. You Know What Your Truth Is – You Always Have, and You Always Will

Your gaslighter doesn't see you.

You are a shadow standing to the side, trying not to attract attention, while they shower their image of you with love and attention. And no matter how much your mind is in knots, you know this to be true.

You know the space you occupy, even if you hate yourself for it. If you look back, if you look inside, you will see that you always knew that something was wrong.

It may feel like you lost your core. But it was always there.

The alarm system always worked. You just learned to stop listening to it. You have not lost as much as you think.

8. The End Game Is Not Confrontation, It's Non-Engagement

A really common trope I see in movies and literature is the survivor who confronts their abuser. They confront them years later, and in that moment show themselves and their abuser that they don't have to be afraid anymore.

I crave that catharsis, because I *am* afraid. But I can never address that fear through confrontation. I can only address it by confidence in my ability to set and enforce my own boundaries.

When you engage in any way, you tell your gaslighter and yourself that your reality is up for debate.

Your reality is not up for debate.

If you're like me, you've had a million conversations in your head, and it's those conversations that are killing you. Your reality is not up for debate. You don't have to rehearse for a conversation that you will never have.

It's ridiculous when someone tries to tell you who you are, what you feel, what you think, what you intended, or what you experienced. When it happens, you should be angry, puzzled, or maybe even concerned for them.

You might stop, stunned, and ask, "What would make you think that you could know what's inside of me? Are you okay?"

Instead, many of us will find ourselves trying to reach understanding.

No, that's not what happened, that's not what I felt, that's not what I feel!

And this is a reasonable response – to a point. But if the goal of the conversation is to exchange power, and not to exchange understanding, you will never, ever, ever win.

I would like to propose that one solution to feeling less susceptible to gaslighting is to learn how to identify the objective of a conversation.

A conversation with the purpose of mutuality should not make you feel afraid, ashamed, disoriented, or confused.

You don't have to figure out what I do think they're doing, you only have to figure out what you are feeling. You only have to know when mutuality is no longer the objective, and learn how to stop engaging when that happens.

Try:

- "We'll have to agree to disagree."
- "I don't like how I feel right now, and I want to finish this conversation later (or never)."
- "What?"
- "You're trying to tell me what my experience is, and I'm not okay with that."
- "Don't contact me again."

"Communicate, communicate, communicate," right? "You can solve anything with enough communication."

That might be a mantra, but it's wrong.

You can solve a lot of things with communication, so long as the objective of both people is understanding. But the minute someone tries to replace your experience, it's time to *stop* communicating, at least on that subject.

9. You Must Confront the Threat

Every gaslighting exchange exists under the shroud of some kind of threat. For my relationship, the threat started out as disapproval, then it was the relationship that was threatened, and eventually the threat escalated to his own life.

I had no ability to confront or resist the gaslighting until one by one, I confronted the fears that these threats produced in me.

I grieved. I spent a week in bed and cried over everything I had poured into the relationship. One by one I tried to internally break my attachments to the things that made me feel trapped.

I cried over the immense shame I felt and tried to build the strength to be able to hold it. First I grieved the family that I wanted so much to be a part of. Then I grieved my relationship with him. Finally, I questioned whether it was right for him to make me responsible for his life. It wasn't easy.

And it was another six months before the relationship ended. But when I realized that I didn't want to be in the relationship anymore, I had already internally confronted the threats that were waiting for me – and as one by one they came out in full force, I was able to put one foot in front of the other and walk out the door.

10. Gaslighting May Be Amplified in Families, Poly Relationships, and Other Groups

It's hard to stand firm when one person is trying to replace your experience, but when they have a chorus of supporters, it is nearly impossible. There is a reason why cult abuse can lead to a complete breakdown of someone's personality.

Group manipulation and abuse is devastatingly effective.

I can't easily explain the level of shame and fear that a group you're deeply invested in can produce with a coordinated attack. We need to be very careful of this in poly groups so we do not exploit this power or unwittingly enable abuse.

I know there is a lot of shame tied up in ending a relationship, and no one wants to be the bad guy. But we all owe it to each other to not participate in relationships where *anyone's* self esteem is being degraded.

It doesn't matter whose fault it is, and it doesn't matter whether or not it is fair. There are bigger things at stake here. Let's not punish each other for doing the things we need to do to be healthy.

...

For more information on gaslighting, or to get support if you or someone you know is being abused, visit the National Domestic Violence Hotline or call 1-800-799-7233.

Please take a quick moment to share here - thanks!

Total Shares 135.3K

RELATED ARTICLES

If You Have Friends and Family Dealing with Substance Abuse and Addiction, Here Are 5 Ways to Support Them

4 Ways Pop Culture Villainizes Modern Women

8 Things White Fans Can Do to Make Fandom More Inclusive

The Gender Playbook: A Guide to Figuring Out Your Non-Binary Identity

WHAT'S HOT RIGHT NOW

3 Ways My Parents Unintentionally Taught Me That My Consent Didn't Matter

5 Microaggressions Secular People Often Hear – And Why They're Wrong

Gaslighting Is a Common Victim-Blaming Abuse Tactic - Here Are 4 Ways to Recognize It in Your Life

4 Reasons Why We Need to Stop Thinking of Skinny-Shaming as 'Reverse Discrimination'

This is What You Need to Catch Everyone's Attention

5 Must Make Moves If You Have An Excellent Credit Score!

This is Scientifically the Most Feel-Good Song Ever Written

Home   Personal Development   Consciousness   Science & Tech   ART   SOCIETY   Health   Quiz   Environment

Home › Consciousness › Self-development
"Gaslighting": One of the Most Dangerous Forms of Mental Manipulation We All Deal With

"GASLIGHTING": ONE OF THE MOST DANGEROUS FORMS OF MENTAL MANIPULATION WE ALL DEAL WITH

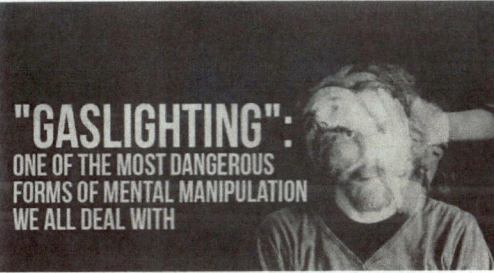

The universe can be a funny place sometimes. I've been doing a lot of research about a form of mental abuse that a lot of us are not only susceptible to, but actually deal with every single day. It is one of those things that we don't even realize is happening to us, we just see the results: self-doubt, diminished self-esteem, and reduced self-worth. The world has a way of beating even the best of us down from time to time but this specific form of manipulation is one that can be identified and removed from our day-to-day existence.

Buy an "Intelligence is sexy" t-shirt!

PLANTED SEEDS OF DOUBT

Back in 1938, there was a play called "Gas Light" that was later adapted into a movie in 1944. In the story, a husband works diligently to convince his wife and their acquaintances that she is insane by making very small and subtle changes to their environment. When the wife would point out the changes, the husband convinced her that she was wrong about the changes and that she was crazy. Slowly but surely, the wife starts to give in to the self-doubt created by those subtle changes, namely a gas lamp that the husband keeps dimming, hence the term "gaslighting".
The Science of Hypnosis

OUR PERCEPTION IS OUR REALITY

In the play, the key was the husband's ability to alter the wife's perception of reality. She saw the lamp as being dimmer and the husband assures her that it is not. He made he doubt her perception, and therefore her reality. It is a form of mental abuse that people too often don't even realize what is happening to them. For the perpetrator, the ability to

RELATED POSTS

CANNABIS OIL HELPS 6-YEAR-OLD GIRL TAKE HER FIRST STEPS ...

Bella Chinonis was born with a very rare medical condition know as "1p36 Depletion Syndrome". This condition is a result of a small amount of genetic material missing from chromosome 1. It's a genetic disorder that can lead to moderate ...

HOW LONG TO NAP FOR THE BIGGEST BRAIN BENEFITS ...

Napping can be great! But sometimes when you wake up after a nap, you feel groggy and almost as if you were more tired now than you were before taking the nap. Why does this happen? According to Dr. Michael ...

control the victim's own perceptions of themselves and the things around them allows them to control the victim themselves. In reality, it happens every single day. It's all around us. How many advertisements do you see that claim that using their product will somehow enhance your life? That's a mild form of gaslighting. You are made to think that some aspect of you or your life is incomplete. You are made to DOUBT yourself. Further, you are made to think that whatever product is being peddled is the solution to what is supposedly lacking in your life.

GASLIGHTING IN OUR LIVES

The specific situation that inspired this article involved one of the most beautiful and amazing women I have ever known dealing with a break up from a man that never deserved to be with her in the first place. I explained to her that there are people in our lives who will try to break us down to be on their level. So, what is the answer to gaslighting?

U.S. Reckoning Day Near

Economist Warns America's Day of Reckoning is Coming. See Proof!

MAINTAINING YOUR OWN REALITY THROUGH YOUR OWN PERCEPTIONS.

I'll tell you now, the same thing I told her:

You see, my friend, there are people in this world who will look at a unicorn and think to themselves, "woah, that is a unicorn, which is something I will never be." They will try to convince you, the unicorn, that you are just an average horse like them with a weird growth on your head that you should probably get checked out by some kind of medical professional that deals with head growths. They will try to steal your magic and make you as dull and ordinary as the plain, old horses that they are. Because they need you to be a plain, old horse like they are, just to bring you down to their level.

The Secrets Behind The Science Of Persuasion

As we've established: you are not just a plain, old horse. You are not a fast race horse. You aren't even one of those fancy British horses that those chicks in those hot pant/knee-high boot getups use to jump over stuff...

YOU ARE A UNICORN. DESPITE WHAT ANYONE ELSE SAYS. YOU ARE ONE IN 7.4 BILLION, AND THAT IS A BEAUTIFUL THING.

27k Shares   G+ Share   Share   Tweet   Pin   Share

COMMENTS

122 comments

4 EVERYDAY ADDICTIONS WE ALL FACE, AND HOW TO OVERCOME THEM ...

Addiction is a very powerful word. It's power comes from the connotations associated with it as they pertain to drugs, alcohol, and destructive behavior in general. People battle with addictions. Addictions ruin lives. In reality, there are addictions all around

35 OF THE BEST "YOGI-ISMS" FROM BASEBALL LEGEND YOGI BERRA ...

Back in September, the world lost baseball legend Yogi Berra who lived to the ripe off age of 90. Berra wasn't only known for his amazing ability on the baseball field that lead to him winning 10 World Series titles

5 AMAZING RESOURCES FOR PERSONAL DEVELOPMENT ...

Personal development is not something that just happens overnight. It is an active pursuit of being the best person you can be, and getting the most out of tis life that you can. You only live once, so squeeze every

RED FLAGGING

Red Flagging occurred *twice* in this case. **First**, improper Treatment Plan that the Doctor patient refused unless made appropriate and safe. **Second**, his academics vs the religious child abuse and criminology in medicine brought into his VA case by VA doctors and the procedure IS NOT MEDICAL but rather a ritual and verified when Elizabeth Joyce Freeman had her phone call with the veteran.

There are times when people need the fear of God instilled. There are different situations. There are different ways. Some more effective than others. And with all cases as two examples below there are times to stay out of things. TO REITERATE: My history with the subject starts with the 1984-1986 Selective Service HIV/AIDS Demographic Study and Vector Analysis as well as the Gilgal Society members who will no longer debate my group members WHO AIDED THE PASSAGE OF THE 1995 Schroeder/Collins Bill H. R. 941 AND ONE DID THAT SURGERY IN 1967 ON A LITTLE 6 YEAR-OLD GIRL IN MY FAMILY. BACK DOWN, BACK AWAY AND FINISH THIS CASE. This is being brought back into the USA again with the new migrants and you are wasting my time.

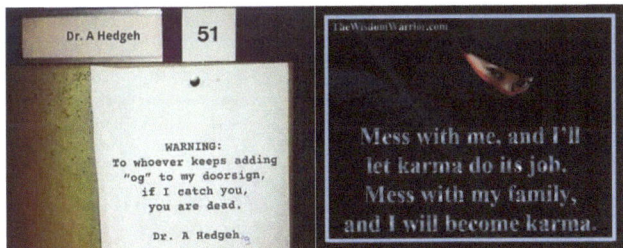

The VA's Infantilized veteran is treated NO DIFFERENT than an abused child:[1]

Child abuse involves every segment of society and crosses all social, ethnic, religious and professional lines. The definition of child abuse can range from a narrow focus, limited to intentional inflicted injury, to a broad scope, covering any act that adversely affects the developmental potential of a child. Included in the definition are neglect (acts of omission) and physical, psychological, or sexual injury (acts of commission) by a parent or caretaker. Intent is not considered in reporting abuse; protection of the child is paramount,... often pursues this practice as a career and will abuse many children over the course of time.

[1] Monteleone, James A., *Recognition of Child Abuse for the Mandated Reporter*, G. W. Medical Publishing, 1996, pp. 1 and 34.

f y 8+ ꓵ ✉   Home » Ben's Blog » Michelle Malkin Exposes Soviet Style VA Flag System

Michelle Malkin Exposes Soviet Style VA Flag System

June 25, 2014 by Benjamin Krause — 19 Comments

DisabledVeterans.Org   Facebook 76   Twitter   Google+ 12   LinkedIn 9   Print 2   Email 1   **100** SHARES

Redeeming The Promise
Of A Square Deal

- Home
- Articles
- About
- Voc Rehab Guide
- Share Your Story
- Contact

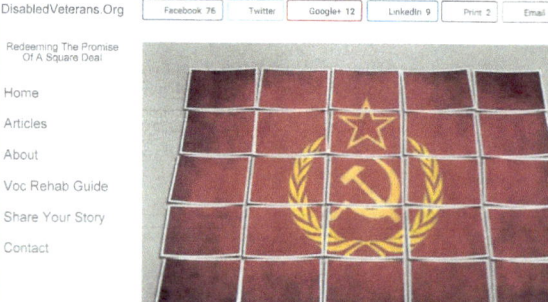

Michelle Malkin of Fox News exposed the scandalous VA flag system using stories of DisabledVeterans.org readers. Malkin reviewed our coverage here of the VA flag system, how it impacts veterans and then called to get the inside scoop.

VA uses secret Disruptive Review Panels that evaluate veteran behavior following complaints from VA employees. The decision of these panels can result in a veteran having their access to health care restricted in a variety of ways. These restrictions range from forcing veterans to embarrassingly check in prior to appointments to flat out refusals of access to health care. The veteran is notified of the flag only after the panel has reached a decision without allowing a due process review by the veteran of the allegations and evidence prior to the administrative procedure. One veteran was informed she was flagged because her health care was too expensive. Outrageous.

Malkin's coverage of this is significant because it gave those of you who reported experiences to me the opportunity to help America learn more about this secret, Soviet-style program once I relayed those experiences on. Malkin was shocked at what she learned – enough so to write about it yesterday.

Disabled Air Force veteran and veterans advocate/attorney Benjamin Krause has been raising questions about the system for months and warning his peers. Under the VA policy on "patient record flags" (PRFs), federal bureaucrats can classify vets as "threats" based on assessments of their "difficult," "annoying" and "non-compliant" behavior.

The VA manual says the flags "are used to alert Veterans Health Administration medical staff and employees of patients whose behavior and characteristics may pose a threat either to their safety, the safety of other patients, or compromise the delivery of quality health care."

That last phrase is priceless. Untold numbers of vets are dead, and legions more have languished because of the VA's failure to deliver "quality health care." The Office of Special Counsel just confirmed to President Obama this week that vets across the country were exposed to contaminated drinking water, dirty surgical tools, untrained doctors and neglectful nurses — and that whistleblowers were retaliated against or ignored.

Yet, the VA's soulless paper-pushers seem more preoccupied with flagging and punishing "disruptive" vets who have dared to complain about their disgraceful treatment and abuse.

One brave veteran is fighting back. Longtime veteran and advocate Lawrence Kelley III was brave enough to come forward for the piece by Malkin. Kelley was helping veterans get educated about their right to sue VA for malpractice by handing out legal fliers at VA – a gutsy move by any estimation.

After VA confronted him for his 1st Amendment speech on federal soil, he was flagged for the legal "threat" he posed. "Once you complain, you are on their hit list forever." Kelley is now challenging the flag due to the VA flag system's unconstitutional nature:

" "This discussion of patient record flags has me fired up," Krause explained. "because of the clear unconstitutional nature of the program. It reminds me of the old Communist techniques used to keep Soviet citizens in check, since I am aware of more than a few veterans who are flagged merely because of their threat to sue VA."

We are going to hold VA accountable and blast their communist system using our laws under the Constitution. Check back soon to see what happens and click below to read more of Michelle Malkin's coverage.

Read More: http://townhall.com/columnists/michellemalkin/2014/06/25/exposed-how-the-va-redflags-disruptive-vets-n1855420/page/full

#####

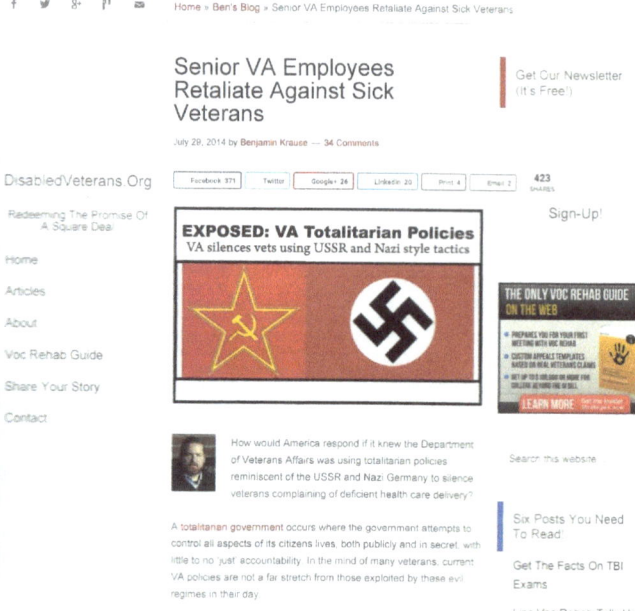

Home » Ben's Blog » Illegal VA Complaints Strategy Against Veterans Exposed

Illegal VA Complaints Strategy Against Veterans Exposed

August 6, 2014 by Benjamin Krause — 61 Comments

DisabledVeterans.Org

Facebook 1k   Twitter   Google+ 36   LinkedIn 49   Print 55   Email 40   **1.2k** SHARES

Redeeming The Promise Of A Square Deal

- Home
- Articles
- About
- Voc Rehab Guide
- Share Your Story
- Contact

Last week, journalist Angela Rae exposed despicable treatment of veterans through a little known process VA employees use against veterans. Some VA employees illegally lodge VA complaints against veterans to manipulate the purpose of disruptive behavior committees.

Angela Rae interviewed me about how veterans are impacted by this illegal retaliation at the receiving end of VA's disruptive behavior committees.

Here is the interview:

It was done via Skype while I was on vacation with family, so the sound has a slight delay. But, you will get a good idea about what is going on and how certain VA doctors and administrators are harming veterans by misusing the process of disruptive behavior committee reviews.

This form of retaliation is, in my opinion, one of the biggest crimes VA is committing across the country because it chills the speech of veterans who respectfully file complaints that have merit. In response to many of these valid complaints, VA employees have been known to file counter complaints that defame the veteran and diminish their credibility. The end result is a veteran having an improper flag on their file, harassment from VA police, and/or restrictions in access to timely health care.

DisabledVeterans.Org
Redeeming The Promise Of A Square Deal

Home
Articles
About
Voc Rehab Guide
Share Your Story
Contact

If you have been harmed by an illegal use of disruptive behavior committee policies, please comment below or send me a private email.

Related

Senior VA Employees Retaliate Against Sick Veterans

Michelle Malkin Exposes Soviet Style VA Flag System

Document Reveals VA Behavior Modification Programs

Filed Under: Ben's Blog
Tagged With: Angela Rae, Complaint, Counter Complaint, Disruptive Behaviors, Filing Complaint, Va Complaints, Va Doctors, Va Employees, Va Police

---

ABOUT BENJAMIN KRAUSE, FOUNDER

Benjamin Krause is a lawyer, investigative reporter and award-winning veterans advocate. He is author of the guide *Voc Rehab Survival Guide for Veterans* and writes every weekday on DisabledVeterans.org. That guide has helped veterans receive millions in retraining and small business support by teaching them how to easily blasting through bureaucratic roadblocks to get their benefits. He

Benjamin Krause – Veteran Challenges from DC Breakdown on Vimeo.

Angela Rae is a sharp journalist, and I will hand it to her for covering this issue. Many in this professional have chosen to back off VA police policies and how they harm veterans after area Directors plea with reporters about how shedding light on the harmful policy.

They cry that it will hurt VA in light of the current scandals.

[Read our earlier coverage on Disruptive Behavior Committees]

VA is now penalizing what should be considered protected speech by misrepresenting it as disruptive behavior, according to the reports I have received and analyzed.

Its authority to make regulations that governs "conduct" falls under 38 USC 901. Somehow, VA has gone from basic authority to govern conduct to the creation of secret committees without a single publication that shows the Disruptive Behavior Committees are working and/or justifiable. In fact, a recent OIG report concluded the committee rules are too vague to be properly applied across VA nationwide. OIG further reported statistics that indicate local administrators are abusing the flexibility of the program granted by the Secretary to manage local issues, much like the wait list scandal.

[Download VA OIG Report on Disruptive Behavior Committees]

How Disruptive Behavior Committees Work In A Nutshell

The reality is that VA has implemented a health care flagging system that illegally restricts the liberty of many veterans without trial. The restriction prevents veterans from easily accessing their right to health care whenever the need arises. Only after a secret committee hearing does the veteran find out whether or not they are "guilty" of disrupting business at VA by complaining.

If VA determines you are disruptive, they will send you an ambiguous letter that does not indicate the law, evidence or who the judge and jury were. The penalty may go on for a year or longer, so in many ways it resembles probation for criminals. However, at least criminals are given a chance to defend themselves prior to being found guilty through a trial.

Usually, the veteran then is required to check in with VA police, and he/she is only able to step on VA property if they have an appointment. There are no emergency services for these individuals, and further no access to veteran organizations housed within the VA facility since they do not take appointments, either. Some veterans are flatly prohibited from seeking VA health care all together without being given any other option.

In many instances, these secret hearings curiously occur after a veteran complains about poor VA health care. In the instances I have covered, a sick veteran first makes a complaint against a VA director or doctor for failing to treat. If VA determines the complaint is angry and hostile (the veteran is usually sick and/or in pain when the complain is made), they will likely flag the veteran by filing their own complaint rather than using common sense to assess the situation.

What we have here is a situation where VA senior managers abuse their police power in retaliation against sick veterans seeking care who file complaints after being victimized by VA, much like agency whistleblowers.

These veterans get none of the privileges and rights afforded common criminals. VA health care professionals have bragged that "This is not your father's VA," but just what kind of new VA is this exactly?

An answer can be found in recent headlines. Secret trials. No rights. Illegal wait lists. Retaliation against dissenters. Ballooning bureaucracy. No accountability. Rampant criminal behavior that kills and injures veterans.

This "new VA" resembles nothing less than Stalin's secret committees in the USSR and Hitler's tribunals in Nazi Germany. There was no oversight and victims of the policies had no chance at a fair shoot at getting justice.

Here, in many instances, the same veterans who are persecuted for speaking out are the same soldiers credited with taking down those oppressive regimes and the criminal tactics they used to silence dissenters. How ironic?

One Real World Example From A Veteran Victimized By Bay Pines VA Medical Center

Take a look at one real sample Disruptive Behavior Committee letter to a veteran found "guilty" of speaking out from Bay Pines VA Medical Center. This veteran gave me permission to publicize his story, but I did opt to remove some specific identifying information from his DBC letter.

The veteran lodged a complaint after being denied care for seven months and after being denied an opportunity to meet with the director of the facility to lodge his complaint directly. He wrote me saying:

> " I was speaking to the Primary Care Nurse Brenda Williams, I requested talking to the director. She informed me the director (Ms. Suzanne Klinker) did not meet with veterans at the VA. I was amazed. I told the Nurse I would meet her for breakfast, lunch of dinner, at Waffle House McDonald's, my house or her house.
>
> I guess this is why the agents came to my residence and I was flagged.

After he said this to the nurse, the veteran reported that VA police stormed his home. He recorded the event on his cell phone, but the police then came over to him, took the phone, and deleted the evidence of their intrusion. They told the veteran he may be arrested and that his claims moving forward would all be "slow walked."

Apparently, "slow walked" is a common term used by VA against veterans who stand up for themselves.

Now, a competent professional would be able to determine that seven months of denials of health care was likely behind the veteran's offer to meet the director wherever she would meet him since she refused to do her job at VA. Thus, the veteran was not a threat to anyone but merely desperate for health care.

Since the police action, the director did agree to speak with the veteran directly and he lodged a complaint with her. Only later did the veteran learn he was flagged after he filed the complaint.

DisabledVeterans.Org

Redeeming The Promise Of A Square Deal

Home

Articles

About

Voc Rehab Guide

Share Your Story

Contact

Toward the middle of the first page of his flag letter, it reads, "VA staff members, and other veterans, have a right to expect to be treated with respect and courtesy in a safe environment." It also indicates the veteran was flagged in the past, though he denies knowledge of this. Now, why does VA not apply their own rules their own employees? If what the veteran has reported is accurate, it is a clear violation of his right to free speech and to a fair evidentiary trial to ensure his speech was truly threatening, at all.

[Download PDF Disruptive Behavior Committee letter]

Questions About Disruptive Behavior Committees

And what about veterans? Are bad doctors flagged so that veterans can know if their doctor has received complaints? Or, is this a one way mirror scheme like at a cop shop for interrogation purposes?

Can you believe it? After your sacrifice, you are now squaring off against the same oppressive totalitarian policies you fought to destroy merely by complaining at a VA health care facility?

And this flagging scheme is not the only one out there. Another lawyer told me he is aware of a few different flagging systems VA uses that could result in harm to a veteran if they speak out or sue VA after an adverse event.

| Facebook 371 | Twitter | Google+ 26 | LinkedIn 20 | Print 4 |
| Email 2 | 423 SHARES |

Related

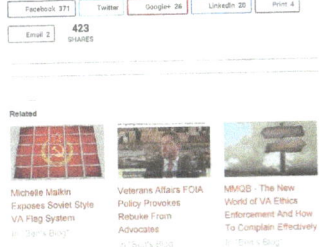

Michelle Malkin Exposes Soviet Style VA Flag System
In "Ben's Blog"

Veterans Affairs FOIA Policy Provokes Rebuke From Advocates
In "Ben's Blog"

MMQB - The New World of VA Ethics Enforcement And How To Complain Effectively
In "Ben's Blog"

Filed Under: Ben's Blog, Veteran Health Care, Veterans Rights

IV: VA After Action Report to Robert McDonald and Linda Spoonster Schwartz

CDR Richard L. Matteoli, DC, USN (ret.), FMF

CONTENT

HISTORY - 2
Positives <-> Negatives

CLAIMS AND CLINICAL RECOMMENDATIONS - 3-5
VA <-> DoD

METHODOLOGY - 6
-> Interdisciplinary <-

ANALYSIS: *FIXING VETERANS HEALTH CARE* **- 7**
Advantages <-> Disadvantages

STRATEGIC AND TACTICAL RECOMMENDATIONS - 8-11
Redirection in DoD Tricare Consolidation then Outward into Reserves and USPH

Conclusion - 12
Invictus

HISTORY

Positives in Part

I am a Mandated Reporter with Prior Notice Given to VA
Confrontation of my Mortality
Taking Control of my Health Care
Learning Impropriety of VA Medical Paternalism
Knowing Propriety of Patient Preference
Criminal Impropriety of Veterans Affairs
Ineffectiveness of VA Improvement
Why VA Director "Generals" Fall on their Swords
Unintended Education
Formulation for VA Procedural Improvement
Formulation for VA, DoD and Civilian Structural Improvement
Wife Medical Transcriptionist
Wife Verbatim Court Reporter
Wife Child Abuse Investigator for Oregon PD
Brother California State Inspector in Enforcement often with AG Attorneys
Veteran Brother-in-Law California State Psychiatric Social Worker
What it took to get this far

Negatives in Part

What it took to get this far
Lost 4 years pay Supplemental Disability Insurance Policy
Lost Life Insurance Policy
Lost Indian Health Retirement
Lost Opportunities
Lost over 10 years of Productive Life
Lost over 10 years Quality Life
Negatively Impacted my Health with Forced Improper Living Conditions
The Sense of VA Infamnia and Vergogna
Marital and Family Discord ***Until Retaliation***

CLAIMS AND CLINICAL RECOMMENDATIONS

1: VA needs to incorporate Shared Responsibility in Veteran Disability Claim decisions.
    a: In Separation of Claimant life experiences sharing claim disability.
    b: In Consolidation of Service Connected disability with shared multiple effects.
2: VA needs to *impress* Shared Responsibility back onto DoD when indicated.

Examples for Success

1: Hearing Loss and Tinnitus
    a: Eliminating VA Testing Standards Impropriety until Rectified.
    b: Refining VA Impropriety with Rectifying Judicial Action through Separation.
2: Aortic Valve Stenosis: Rheumatic Heart
    a: Omit naming El Toro and Lejeune; otherwise, note not a Base Contamination issue.
    b: Reference as Boot Camp and Large Clinic situations with high transient populations.
3: Heavy Metal Mercury Poisoning with Rectifying Judicial Action through Consolidation.
    a: Omit naming El Toro and Lejeune; otherwise, not a Base Contamination issue.
    b: Stress Pre 1980 Dentistry prior to advanced techniques and materials.
4: Tuberculosis: Impress Initial Responsibility back onto DoD.

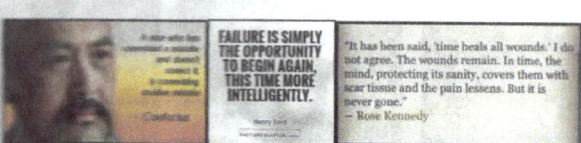

3

VA Legal Responsibility: Standards of Care and Diagnostics

1: The VA is open to more Class Action and Individual Law Suits including Criminal Behavior.
2: Lost Life Insurance and Indian Health Retirement rests on 10% each for Hearing Loss and Tinnitus.
3: Lost Supplemental Disability Insurance and all incurred costs rests on Heart, Mercury and TB.
4: All else, including Retaliation, rests on VA response to other than specific medical conditions.

 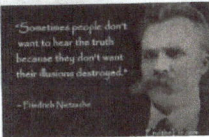 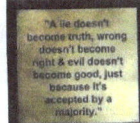

Hearing Loss and Tinnitus

Hearing Loss: Shared Responsibility

1: Establish Legal International Usual and Customary Diagnostic Testing for Auditory Pathology to 8000 Hz.
2: Maintain Hearing Aid Standards to 4000 Hz.
3: Use Graph Similar to Example Photo.
4: Make Graph Overlay for each year of life.
5: Graph Overlay to Include *Range of Normalcy*.
6: Hearing Loss Greater than Range of Normalcy is Pathology.
7: Establish if Service Connection Applies.
8: Establish Claimant Lifestyle.
9: Establish Percent (%) Shared Responsibility if applies.
10: Shared Responsibility can be calculated as 50% Equity.

Tinnitus: Shared Responsibility

1: Determine Severity of Tinnitus affecting Cognitive Hearing Loss.
2: Establish Claimant Lifestyle and Truthfulness.
3: Establish Percent (%) Shared Responsibility if applies.
4: Shared Responsibility can be calculated as 50% Equity.

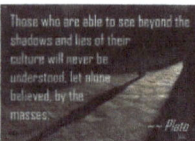 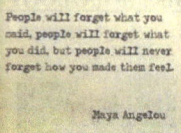 

Aortic Valve Stenosis: Rheumatic Heart

1: Be straightforward and honest in everything. (*The VA is Killing and Euthanizing my Troops at Home*).
2: Decent Cardiologists know the difference between Aortic Valve Stenosis and Endocarditis.
3: Do not allow obfuscation with a *Misdirection* False Argument in diagnostic denial making the veteran jump through another hoop where in my case it has been almost a decade of active conflict.
4: If a Claimant brings their Military Medical Record and/or Social Security Disability Exam say so and read them, not just *He brought his papers* and not want to look at them. (The Podiatrist at the VA Hospital; San Francisco read them catching the 1986 *Military rampant Misdiagnosing and Avoidance*).
5: Do not mention military instillations subject to Base Contamination issues unless appropriate.
6: Note **a)** Date of Diagnosis on RAD physical, 1991; and, **b)** *Date of Correct Diagnosis, 2005.*
7: My case should be written for 20% noting it is a Progressive Disease.

Mercury Poisoning: Disease Consolidation

1: *Consolidate all other resulting health issues from this contamination into one disability.*
2: Note, in my case, my 5 years active duty in Boot Camps between 1971 – 1986.
3: Note materials used in dentistry advanced and we no longer work with liquid mercury.
4: Note the effects are *Latent* and often takes years to present pathologically.
5: My case should be written for 30% thus giving VA 10% incremental Equity Shared Responsibility.

Tuberculosis: Now Will NOT Monetarily Affect the VA

1: Note Diabetes diagnosis on September 2000 requiring prophylaxis due to my profession.
2: Note VA assumed responsibility from Date of Retirement on 18 April 2005.
3: Note VA commenced treatment when **able to properly do so** on 01 November 2010 which removes professional disability to Service Connected 0% (Zero) unless TB becomes active.
4: This will be 100% either as: **a)** September 2000 to November 2010; or, **b)** 18 April 2005 through 01 November 2010. (*ASIDE*: My attorney prefers the former with this packet finalized as above in order to alter my Focus of Attention next in giving appropriate Notice to DoD and BUMED/FORCEMED).

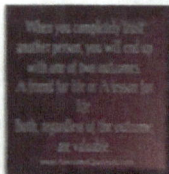  

METHODOLOGY

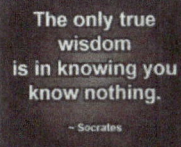

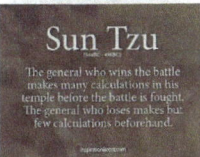

Interdisciplinary in Part

Forensic Cultural Anthropology
Medicine
Criminology
Munchausen Complex
Malignant Narcissism
Freudian Singularity
Emma Jung Duality
Carl Jung Duality
Transactional Analysis
Nature of the Ego
Psychosexual Communication
Communicative Theology
Jungian Tetrads
False Arguments
Propaganda Techniques
Persuasion Analysis
Public Relations
Archetypical Dimensions
Psychosexual Deifications
Mythic Expressions
Psychosexual Sociopathy
Sacrifice - Euthanasia

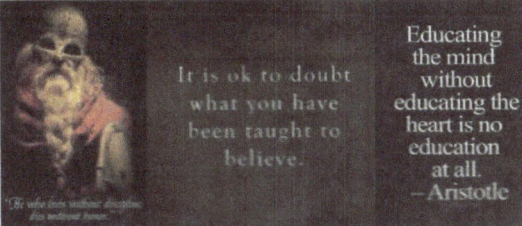

ANALYSIS: *FIXING VETERANS HEALTH CARE*

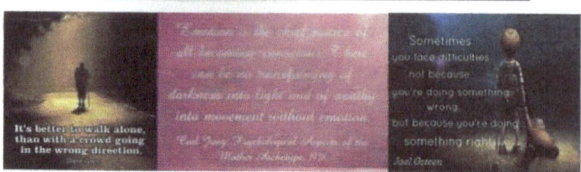

In relation to Health Care Force Integration through Tricare Consolidation

In Part:

Advantages

Addresses Acute Need for New Direction of VA
Illustrates Necessity of Interagency and Interdisciplinary Cohesion
VA to Clinically Treat Only Service Connected Disability Patients
Redirects Past VA *Mission Creep* Toward Proper Alternatives
Examples Logistic Inabilities to Health Care Delivery
Logistic Complications Unduly Increase VA Costs
Links Alternative Insurance Needs for Veterans
Links Veterans to Civilian Sector Health Care Delivery
Gives Solution to Long Term Care Needs

Disadvantages

Maintains and Increases Separation
Creates New Bureaucracy
More Subject to Improper Political Introjection
More Subject to Improper Business Introjection
Omits Facility Sharing with Civilian Sector
Omits Facility Sharing with Other Governmental Agencies
Does Not Link R&D with Civilian Sector
Eliminates Veteran Option for VA and Civilian Medical Health Care Sharing
Does not Link VA with DoD in Shared Concerns
Does not Link VA with DoD Past, Present and Future Assets
DOES NOT ADDRESS NATIONAL FORCE READINESS REQUIREMENTS

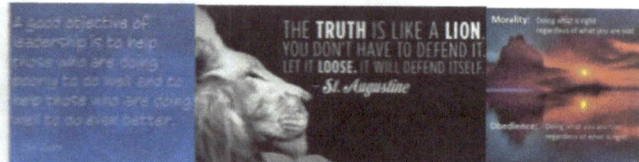

STRATEGIC AND TACTICAL RECOMMENDATIONS

IT IS ESSENTIAL TO SOAR AS AN EAGLE RATHER THAN HIDE LIKE A TURTLE IN ITS SHELL

Redirection in DoD Tricare Consolidation then Outward into Reserves, USPHS and DHHS

STRATEGIC PURPOSE	TACTICAL CONCERNS
Rectify Immediate Concerns	Enhance Public Safety
Seek Future Opportunities	Overturn Financial Losses
Truthful Situational Communications	Restore Lost Reputation

LOGISTICS and SUPPLY

All Fixed Assets Exist
All Non-Fixed Assets Exist
All Consumables Available
Internet Communications Functioning
All Patient Records Exist
All Health Care Providers Vetted
All Support Personnel Available
All First Responders Vetted
All Business Providers Vetted
All Transportation Available
All Security Functioning

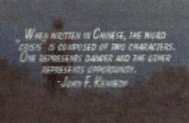

Phase I: STRATEGY and TACTICS

Congressional Approval for Tricare Exists

Encompass		Penetrate
Review Congressional Approval		Mobilize VA First
Develop Battle Plan		Interagency Coordination
Reaches All Societal Aspects		Agencies Step Mobilize
Provide Proper Health Care		Electronic Transfer
Increases National Security		Secure Records Each Agency
Tricare Exists Unto Itself		Repeat in Orderly Expansion
Total Encompassment		Sectional Penetrations

Phase II: INTEGRATION within VA

Strategic Acute Initial Necessity with Tactical Development

Maintain Focus on Treating Service Connected Disabilities
Upgrade then Maintain Increased Reserve Readiness
Maximize Shared Civilian Health Care Assets and Cooperation
Maximize Educational Health Care Assets
Eliminates Majority Travel Reimbursements and Eliminates Other Ancillary Expenses
Cover: Administrative, Congressional and Judicial Branches of Government
Veteran Source for Qualified Reenlistments and Recalls who are Medical-Dental Ready

Phase III: INTEGRATION with DoD

Consolidation and Expansion of Force Elements in National Security

Penetration Through VA
Coordinate Reserve Health Care
Coordinate National Guard Health Care
DIA, NSA, NGA, NRO, DSS, etc.
DARPA, DLA, MDA, DTRA, PFPA, DTIC, etc.
Coordinate CIA, DOJ, DHS, ATF, TSA, NASA, etc.
Coordinate with Selective Service
USO Ancillary Support

Phase IV: INTEGRATION with USPHS

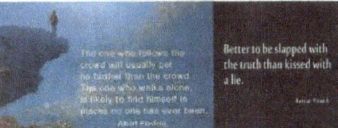

Consolidates Non DoD Assets Transferrable into DoD During National Emergency

Penetration Through DoD
US Coast Guard
National Oceanic and Atmospheric Administration
Bureau of Indian Affairs
National Institute of Health
Federal Prison Personnel Assets
Centers of Disease Control and Prevention
FEMA Support Elements
Food and Drug Administration
Centers for Medicare and Medicaid Services
Move DHS and INS into USPHS

10

Phase V: UNITY of COMMAND and DHHS

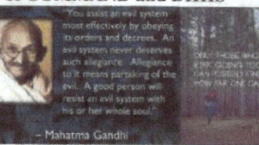

Cover Additional Agencies with MOS Equivalency for National Emergency

Penetration Through USPHS
Federal, State, County, District
Corporate, Non Profit, Business, Private

Phase VI: REMOVES OBAMACARE IMPROPRIETIES

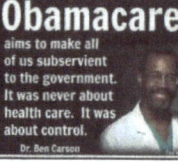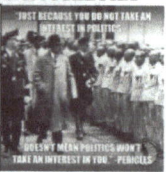

Puts Health Care where it belongs NOT with the IRS

Eliminates Possibility of Saudi Microchip with WiFi activating lethal dose added
Eliminates coverage for the Death Penalty
Eliminates Politically Favorable Exemptions
Reduces Contractual Fraud
Removes Mandatory Participation with Penalties
Provider and Patient Equality
Eliminates Stagnation of Treatment to Allow Industry Standards of Treatment Upgrades

11

CONCLUSION

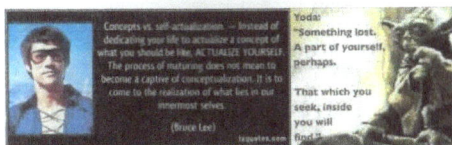

SEIZE OBJECTIVES NOW - DEFEND GAINS AFTER

Existing Disunity
Cyclic *Molon Labe*

Currently the VA has a system that relies on the If-Then structure of a Circular Argument through shouting *Molon Labe* at each other as if each speaks with the defiant authority of Leonidas in the attitude of "Come and Take It" in each step taken by both perceiving success in a *Carpe Diem* of "Seize the Day. Excellent, but **only when** *individually* and *socially* **appropriate**. Elan:

Essential Spirit

**There is no sin in falling.
Sin is in not getting up and moving forward.
Arise with inner Spirit. Left foot first.
Never stop. Never quit. If tired, walk… Crawl.**
Col. Gerald Fink, (*POW, DC*),USMC

Necessitated Unity
Shared *Invictus*

Invictus, the result of successful and proper Molon Labe by an *individual*, is illustrated by Airman Sgt. James Cook saluting the Stars and Stripes upon return from the Hanoi Hilton, Vietnam:

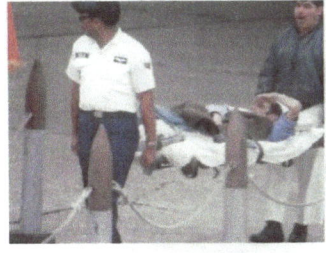

Educational Aids
In order of Appearance

[1] *Molon Labe*, "Come and Take Them," Leonidas, King of Sparta.

[2] *Carpe Diem*, "Seize the Day," Horace, *Odes*, Book 1, Number 11.

[3] *Molon Labe*, "Come and Take Them," Leonidas, King of Sparta.

[4] Eye of Ra and Horus. (Archetypical Dimension. Mythic Expression).

[5] Archetypical Dimension; Mythic Expression.

[6] Eye of Ra and Horus. (Archetypical Dimension. Mythic Expression).

[7] *You can ignore reality, but you cannot ignore the consequences of ignoring reality*, Ayn Rand.

[8] *If you can't be safe – Be deadly.*

[9] *Do not regret the fight. Pity those that never knew the privilege of it.*

[10] *They must find it difficult… those who have taken authority as truth, rather than truth as authority*, Gerald Massey.

[11] Fallen Warrior Totem.

[12] *Warriors confront the evil that most people refuse to acknowledge.* Bohdi Sanders.

[13] *If you expect the world to be fair with you because you are fair, you're fooling yourself. That's like expecting the lion to you because you didn't eat him.* (A Totemic Analogy: Simile).

[14] *The cave you fear to enter holds the treasure that you seek.* Joseph Campbell.

[15] *It is easier to build strong children than to repair broken men.* Frederick Douglass.

[16] *If your actions do not prove the truth of your words, then your words are nothing more than lies.* Ritu Ghatourey.

[17] *The most dangerous liars are those who think they are telling the truth.*

[18] *Sometimes you have to give up on people. Not because you don't care, but because they don't.*

[19] *A man who has committed a mistake and doesn't correct it, is committing another mistake.* Confucius.

[20] *Failure is simply the opportunity to begin again, this time more intelligently.* Henry Ford.

[21] *It has been said, 'time heals all wounds.' I do not agree. The wounds remain. In time, the mind, protecting its sanity, covers them with scar tissue and the pain lessens. But it is never gone."* Rose Kennedy. (Within the Wounded Child Archetype).

[22] *We're all in the same game; Just different levels. Dealing with the same hell; just different devils.*

[23] *Sometimes people don't want to hear the truth because they don't want their illusions destroyed.* Friedrich Nietzsche.

[24] *A lie doesn't become truth, wrong doesn't become right and evil doesn't become good, just because it's accepted by the majority.*

[25] Audiogram example.

[26] *When a well-packaged web of lies has been sold gradually to the masses over generations, the truth will seem utterly preposterous and its speaker a raving lunatic.* Dresden James.

[27] *Be not the slave of your own past. Plunge into the deep and swim far. So you shall come back with self-respect, with new power, with an advanced experience that shall explain and overlook the old.* Ralph Waldo Emerson.

[28] *If you succeed in cheating someone, Don't think that the person is a fool... Realize that the person trusted you much more than you deserved... It.* Nishan Panwar.

[29] *Those who are able to see beyond the shadows and lies of their culture will never be understood, let alone believed, by the masses.* Plato.

[30] *People will forget what you said, people will forget what you did, but people will never forget how you made them feel.* Maya Angelou.

[31] *The illerate of the 21st Century will not be those who cannot read and write, but those who cannot learn, unlearn, and relearn.* Alvin Toffler.

[32] *When you completely trust another person, you will end up with one of two outcomes. A friend for life or a lesson for life. Both, regardless of the outcome, are valuable.*

[33] *There comes a time when you have to stop crossing oceans for people who wouldn't jump puddles for you.*

[34] *Sometimes you have to move on without certain people. If they're meant to be in your life, they'll catch up.* Mandy Hale.

[35] *The only true wisdom is in knowing you know nothing.* Socrates.

[36] *Sometimes you fall down because there is something down there that you are supposed to find.*

[37] *The general who wins the battle makes many calculations in his temple before the battle is fought. The general who loses makes but few calculations beforehand.* Sun Tzu.

[38] *The goal of life is not t5o join the majority but to escape the ranks of the insane.* Marcus Aurelius.

[39] *He who lives without discipline dies without honor.* Icelandic Proverb.

[40] *It is OK to doubt what you have been taught.*

[41] *Educating the mind without educating the heart is no education at all.* Aristotle.

[42] *It's better to walk alone, than with a crowd going in the wrong direction.* Diane Grant.

[43] *Emotion is the chief source of all becoming ~ conscious. There can be no transforming of darkness into light and of apathy into movement without emotion.* Carl Jung, "Psychological Aspects of the Mother Archetype," 1938.

[44] *Sometimes you face difficulties not because you are doing something wrong, but because you are doing sometimes right.* Joel Osteen.

[45] *A good objective of leadership is to help those who are doing poorly to do well and to help those who are doing well to do even better.* Jim Rohn.

[46] *The truth is like a lion. You don't have to defend it. Let it loose. It will defend itself.* St. Augustine.

[47] **Morality:** Doing what is right regardless of what you are told. **Obedience:** Doing what you are told regardless of what is right.

[48] *Imagine a new story for your life and start living it.* Paulo Coelho.

[49] *You must give up the life you planned in order to have the life that is waiting for you.* Joseph Campbell.

[50] *Do not go where the path may lead, go instead where there is no path and leave a trail.* Ralph Waldo Emerson.

[51] *I can always make it a rule to get there first with the most men.* Nathan Bedford Forrest.

[52] *Sometimes your only available transportation is a leap of faith.* Margaret Shepard.

[53] *In the middle of every difficulty lies opportunity.* Albert Einstein.

[54] *When written in Chinese, the word "crisis" is composed of two characters. One represents danger and the other represents opportunity.* John F. Kennedy.

[55] *If you know the enemy a know yourself, you need not fear the result of a hundred battles.* Sun Tzu.

[56] Dear Optimist, Pessimist, and Realist,… While you guys were busy arguing about the glass of water, I drank it… Sincerely, The Opportunist.

[57] *Strategy without Tactics is the slowest route to victory. Tactics without Strategy is the noise before defeat.* Sun Tzu.

[58] Elements of Strategy and Tactics.

[59] *Those who are skilled in combat do not become angered, those who are skilled at winning do not become afraid. Thus the wise win before the fight, while the ignorant fight to win.* O Sensei Ueshiba.

[60] *The warrior who trusts his path doesn't need to prove the other is wrong.* Paulo Coelho.

[61] *In a military operation, the command and control elements are a legitimate target.* Stephen Hadley.

[62] *Care about what other people think and you will always be their prisoner.* Lao Tzu.

[63] *Strong convictions precede great actions.* James Freeman Clarke.

[64] Seal: Joint Chiefs of Staff.

[65] Seal: Combined Arms Center; Special Troops Battalion. USA.

[66] *The one who follows the crowd will usually get no further than the crowd. The one who walks alone, i8s likely to find himself in places no one has ever been.* Albert Einstein.

[67] *Better to be slapped with the truth than kissed with a lie.* Russian Proverb.

[68] *In the middle of every difficulty lies opportunity.* Albert Einstein.

[69] *Do not blame Caesar, blame the people of Rome who have rejoiced in their loss of freedom who hail him when he speaks in the Forum of more security, more living fatly at the expense of the industrious.* Marcus Cicero.

[70] *You assist an evil system most effectively by obeying its orders and decrees. An evil system never such allegiance. Allegiance to it means partaking of the evil. A good person will resist an evil system with his or her whole soul.* Mahatma Gandhi.

[71] *Only those who will risk going too far can possibly find out how far one can go.* T. S. Eliot.

[72] *Nothing just happens in politics. If something happens, you can be sure it was planned that way.* The Penguin. (Film).

[73] *Obamacare aims to make all of us subservient to the government. It was never about health care. It was about control.* Dr. Ben Carson.

[74] *Just because you do not take an interest in politics... Doesn't mean politics won't take an interest in you.* Pericles.

[75] *Those who can make you believe absurdities can make you commit atrocities.* Voltaire.

[76] *The strictest law sometimes becomes the severest injustice.* Benjamin Franklin.

[77] *Don't wait for the perfect moment; Take the moment and make it perfect.* Zoey Sayward.

[78] (Concepts vs. Self-actualization). *Instead of dedicating your life to actualize a concept of what you should be like, actualize yourself. The process of maturing does not mean to become a captive of conceptualization. It is to come to the realization of what lies in our innermost selves.* Bruce Lee.

[79] *Something lost. A part of yourself, perhaps. That which you seek, inside you will find.* Yoda. (Film). (Archetypical Dimension. Mythic Expression).

[80] *My life is so much more interesting inside my head.*

[81] *Molon Labe*, "Come and Take Them," Leonidas, King of Sparta.

[82] Photo: Airman Sgt. James Cook.

[83] *INVICTUS*, William Ernest Henley.

III: VA GOMER Recommendations to Robert McDonald and Linda Spoonster Schwartz

CDR Richard L. Matteoli, DC, USN (ret.), FMF

May this addendum regarding VA *Forensic Cultural Anthropology* prove helpful to all, in their own particular way, who are involved in the quest for the expansion of *VA improvement*.

 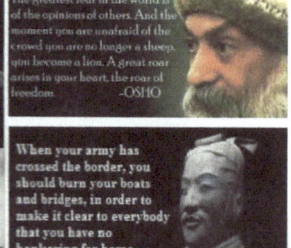 

MANAGERIAL RESPONSIBILITY

Veterans Affairs has a criminal history expressing many types of Patterns of Behavior. Behaviors appear to be individual, others Team Predation. Militarily, they must be considered as Traitors or Rogue Units. It became incumbent for the OIG to give Loma Linda education on Criminology. This would be appropriate for all management levels within the VA because it has become inherent, to some points acculturated. Regardless of position of employment, power is given. Power can corrupt. Power is addictive. Power must be maintained in criminal endeavors; thus, other behaviors arise to ensure continuance as finding excuses to justify which themselves increase the degree of Criminology. Drunkenness in power creates Hubris. Hubris becomes the downfall of a mythic hero to even the individual. Initial recommendations are:

HEARING LOSS – Acculturated Criminology; Improperly Crossed Border

The Hearing Aid test to 4000Hz is *only* set to hearing loss requiring mechanical assistance, NOT totally inclusive as a Diagnosis to all Auditory Pathology. This defect is acculturated. Usual and Customary Standard of Care diagnosing hearing loss pathology inclusively extends to all points that reach 8000Hz. Anything else constitutes a violation of the Service Member's *Contract Intent* with the United States government and actionable as such.

Necessity

1). Establish proper testing procedures for Diagnosing Hearing Loss Pathology according to International Usual and Customary Standards of Care not a point but rather a Range Of Normalcy including 4000Hz through 8000Hz. A graph can be made as a Guideline for determining claim validity.
2). Make a Public Service Announcement that veterans declined may reapply to have their case reviewed.
3). Have Auditory Resources update their Conference Packet.

Recommendation

The VA is building a new clinic in my Monterey. Part of its existing facility can be converted as a separate temporary section to review Hearing Loss Claims and Tinnitus if included and appropriate. To do otherwise would place too much a burden on existing VBA Regions. All bonuses should be terminated and directed to resolving this with, by, new hires.

TINNITUS

There is no test specific for Tinnitus. It can be diagnosed by the temporary Tinnitus Notch that occurs in the 3000Hz range and subsides over time toward the 2000Hz Range. Do not know if pathology persists after subsiding. Everyone most likely has multiple single instances to including combinations of factors, some long term. Tinnitus for disability relies on patient honesty.

Did not acquire the helicopter MRO for my Hearing Loss and Tinnitus. Did not know it exists. Felt could not prove the occurrence. Had to dismiss and concentrate on the facts of my profession, especially the first half of my Navy Career. Learned of the MRO from my Disabled American Veterans VA Representative on 23 September 2014. Mercury poisoning is latent. Existence MRO *verified* by CAPT Thomas Walczyk, DC, USN, (ret.), friend since Great Lakes and aided him on ADSW at Top Gun, Fallon. They let him fly training 2nd seat, Code Name -> *Jawbreaker*. *My Lesson Learned*.

Request: VA Obtain Helicopter MRO

Please attain the Helicopter Maintenance, Repair and Overhaul (MRO) for that helicopter. Was sitting in the middle directly under the engine when it blew. It was before my TB diagnosis in late 1998 while being evacuated from Tooksook Bay, Alaska coincidentally where I contacted TB. My attempts to contact have failed. Location: Alaska National Guard DMVA; Bethel Readiness Center. [Enclosures].

2

AORTIC VALVE STENOSIS and Procedure Codes

Denial is based on a *Misdiagnosis*. My claim is Procedure Code **7000**, NOT Procedure Code 7001. ***Use them in claims.*** Cardiologists know the difference between Endocarditis and Rheumatic Heart Valve. As the doctor noted, I brought my *paperwork* with me and that my case is good if proven otherwise. Paperwork included my military health record. After being told by a Corpsman the second time he purged my record I checked out my medical record and kept it. The ONLY VA physician that looked at it was for my feet on Appeal. The Cardiologist REFUSED to look at it. What good is an ACTUAL Patient History to the VA?

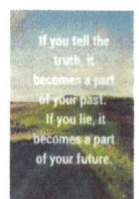

PATIENT HISTORIES SHOULD BE BASED ON A HEALTH QUESTIONAIRRE UPDATED ANNUALLY and have a section with at least 5 years for recall patient Signatures.

Responsibility of those who have the veteran *in the care* of their employment does not reside alone with those giving treatment. Responsibility is as much if not more in those directing and driving policies and procedures whether official policy or unofficial policies which may be contradictory to Veterans Affairs. What are VA ideals? In retrospect it is as if I know when the Cardiologist made his decision as did the doctor on my first visit. It was the similar. Why? Why? Why? ... *My Lesson Learned*.

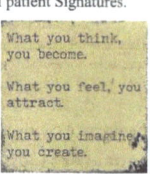

TUBERCULOSIS – Acculturated Criminology; Improperly Crossed Border

(6724, 6731) *not* originally a VA problem. FORCEMED refused to treat though had correct Treatment Plan. Responsibility passed to the VA. VA had correct Diagnosis but improper Treatment Plan. Did not have BUMED Tuberculosis Directives until after getting Social Security Disability, which should become, in its own way, written VA Policy and Procedure. **6724** *requires* stepdown Disability Rating. [Enclosure]

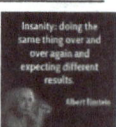

Recommendation: "Collegial" Regional *Pharmacological Discussion Facilities*

Keep *Collegial* in name, but with in-house *Hotline*. VA Pharmacology cannot be sold to a French company. If it could be sized up and as done in the first month by a CEO, such is the *smell* of an excellent Diagnosis and great Treatment Plan. Facility can be set in old Monterey Clinic. *Hasten completion*. See: Hearing Loss, p. 2 and Pharmacology, p. 5. Since Great Lakes 1984-1986 this has been *only talk*. [Enclosure].

Myss relates common Archetypical Dimensions via unconscious Child Archetypes. PTSD requires Betrayal. The Wounded Child requires Humiliation. VA inflicts both. Most disease involves, in some way, Stress. The main Stress causal to many diseases is Monetary. My diabetes was normal for three days after seeing Mr. Evans. *My Lesson Learned*.

3

MERCURY POISONING: INCLUSIVE PARITY and EQUITY

This was a Strategic Reserve to Tactically develop at a later date if felt necessary other to Tinnitus. It is now Deployed back on the table, see: pp. 5 and 10. Sometimes inferiority is true when a person is not in full knowledge. Yet, the serious minded overcomes. *My Lesson Learned*.

Elemental Mercury poisoning is regulated by OSHA. Involves Occupational Exposure with the medium being air via inhalation and absorption pulmonary. Was in denial that amalgam restorations cause Mercury Poisoning and still do not think as serious per-se to the patient. BUT, have overcome denial with regard to Occupational Exposure from FDA document by *Windham*. This is *akin to Nitrous Oxide Sedation* that causes cancer and birth defects from both sexes mainly in Health Care Professionals who use Nitrous Oxide. *My Lesson Learned*.

Recommendation:

Insurance companies employ physicians to review cases as mine and answer questions. This should become a VA Policy and Procedure for Claims Analysts to request and/or have access to for questions. Such physicians are usually retired or somehow physically disabled to continue practice. It appears VA Oakland did all they could to *not* properly Discover. <u>VA is Responsible for Failure to Diagnose</u>. Yet, it was hinted at by Palo Alto but I was re-assigned.

DIABETES (7913) 20% Rate: Again: *My Lesson Learned*. [Enclosure: Diabetes Denial].

ATHEROSCLEROSIS (7005): Ms. Pennington was more correct than all encountered. VA must find which of my records were *Accidentally Lost On Purpose*. Again: *My Lesson Learned*.

MITRAL VALVE (7005): Again: *My Lesson Learned*.

CORONARY (7006): 1970's met Actuarial who said from Stress. Again: *My Lesson Learned*.

THYROID (7901): From this I became Military Non-Qual. But signed waiver at behest of the DoD because of the *Needs of the Navy* for my profession. Class 4 Restrictions included: 1) Loss of Promotions. 2). No Overseas Assignments. [Enclosures]. Again: *My Lesson Learned*.

CHRONIC FATIGUE (7901): Chronic Fatigue may be caused by Mercury Poisoning and indicated in my Social Security Disability Exam. Again: *My Lesson Learned*.

Frankl's quote concerns Human Relations, not fully inclusive to Medical Consequence.

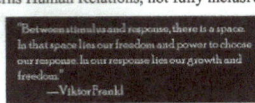

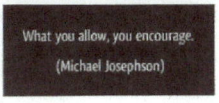
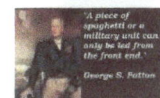

FORTITUDE

Veterans Affairs must take stock of its Policies and Procedures. They are in gross violation of US government *Contract Intent* made with the Veteran. And reachable.

PATIENT and VETERAN RECORDS: DoD and VA

PURGING and MISSING RECORDS: Both the VA and the DoD possess instance of these violations. This is unfair and violates ALL involved: The VA, DoD and Veteran. VA should take the initiative, approach DoD, and resolve the shared problem.

PHARMACEUTICAL: DoD and VA

Follow MSDS International and Industry Safety Standards using the Physician's Desk Reference (PDF). Examples, in part: 1). Tuberculosis Liver Monitoring. 2). Opiates. There was no reason the OIG and Congress needed to investigate San Francisco. [Enclosures].

INCLUSIVE DUTY TO ALL SERVICE MEMBERS: DoD and VA

Follow DoD Directive 1241.1, 28 February 2004. *VA Violation Contract Intent*. There should be NO day requirement other than Day of Occurrence. Suspicions exist. My case is *Death by a Thousand Cuts*. [Enclosure: Diabetes Denial].

PARITY and EQUITY: VA <--> VETERAN: BALANCE

Parity and Equity may use court Precedence of Shared Responsibility. VA Disability Rating is too confined yet Percent Disability within a Category acceptable but needs to Segment the Within and Confine the Outward. The current system creates an *All-or-Nothing* mentality for both the VA and Veteran. Parity and Equity will greatly decrease VA decision conflict. Fairness must mediate. Categories to Segment and Confine, in part to example: 1). Hearing Loss and Tinnitus should Segment at a 5% Shared Responsibility to both Military and Civilian causality. 2). Mercury Poisoning and Heart Disease to Confine the Outward by considering all possible aspects of causality into one rating as: 20% or 30% all indicators combined abating possible future connecting via satisfaction.

5

READING LIST

There is no VA Discipline and it never possessed Unit Cohesion. Command and Control of the mind is lacking. Each Branch of the Service has a Reading List. So too Entertainment Industry scientists. [Enclosures]. Put a secure Kindle Edition of all books, with Myss' *Sacred Contracts* 3rd, in order below left to right, on a disc and give to all Veterans Affairs employees. Flip the Jabba Coin to the Light Side of its Archetypical Dimension. *The Veteran must be heard.*

 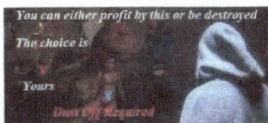 

A Message to Garcia, *Elbert Hubbard.* Orders=Personnel; Message=Job Description; Garcia=Supervisor. Go to work.

Animus and Anima, *Emma Jung.* It's all about sex emanating from the unconscious id. The opposite sex within us. Combined Inherent Difference within each individual. Introduction to the Archetypical Dimension. It's looking out at thee, then looking into me; and, back into thee.

Games People Play, *Eric Berne.* Transactional Analysis (TA) is *Communication.*

On Death and Dying, *Elisabeth Kubler Ross.* Process of Grieving.

Achilles in Vietnam, *Jonathan Shay.* PTSD, Betrayal required, In-Country.

Why Good People Do Bad Things, *James Hollis.* Criminology. *Everybody's* Dark Side.

On Grief and Grieving, *Elisabeth Kubler Ross.* Wounds deep, continuance psychic infliction.

Odysseus in America, *Jonathan Shay.* PTSD, Betrayal, End In-Country through Lifetime.

The Nazi Doctors: Genocide and the Psychology of Medical Killing, *Robert Lifton.* Doubling. One must learn the difference between *Doubling* and *Constructive Displacement.*

RESOLUTION
WHO WHAT WHEN WHERE and HOWEVER:
THE "WHY" IS EVIDENT. MOVE OUT; GET 'ER DONE.

Veterans Affairs is in dire need of a Publicity Campaign. It can be initiated with one well-coordinated event. A select group of Veterans must engage support. Only need to be contacted. Combined Force Evolution. Chesty Puller's ONE is the Veteran. Template for whatever you choose.

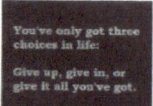

If you choose to accept, I will assist. Battalion Aid Station requesting orders giving total Authority to Dust Off to Lace Up until Inspection Ready. Dust Off will coordinate with USMC Quantico counterpart. Civilians would be accessed through my personal friend/Entertainment Attorney whose father was a Marine Chosin Reservoir survivor. If felt acceptable will give permission to use my case, anonymously because of specific patient content, as a Training Aide. Something, anything, is needed. These Mandated Reports are your FFP. Go deeper with more *Pattern Analysis*.

Request: Colonel Wayne Rich, JAG, USMC, (Ret.); DOJ, (Ret.)

Served with Colonel Wayne Rich during our Desert Storm recalls at Marine Corps Air Station, El Toro. He would be best to Collegially bridge legality and VA Criminology. [Enclosures].

7

MILITARY HEALTH CARE HISTORY

Health Care Professionals are Geneva Code Non Combatants; BUT, allowed to take arms especially under patient and facility duress and join the fight if possible. The VA represents a civilian counterpart and reachable through the courts. A plaque of Medal of Honor recipients and selected others should be placed in clinical settings to give VA personnel identity with service personnel that have shared their profession. Selected examples, in part, include just some Medal of Honor recipients:

Capt. Ben Salomon
DC, USA, WWII

Lt Jg. Alexander Lyle
DC, USN[MC], WWI

Lt Jg. Weeden Osborne,
DC, USN[MC], WWI

3rd Class Richard DeWert
Corpsman, USN[MC], Korea

3rd Class Edward Benfold
Corpsman, USN[MC], Korea

3rd Class William Charette
Corpsman, USN[MC], Korea

3rd Class John Kilmer
Corpsman, USN[MC], Korea

HN Francis Hammond
Hospitalman, USN[MC], Korea

Lt Jg. John Koelsch, Pilot
USN, Hilo Med Evac, Korea

Sgt. David Bleak
Medic, USA, Korea

Pfc. Bryant Womak
Medic, USA, Korea

Major Charles Loring, USAF
POW Germany WWII, DFC.
Action included: Air-Ground
Support for Med Evac, Korea

OTHER

Military Medicine variously influences many. In 1948 Navy Hospital Corpsmen sub-classified as dental technicians were transferred to Dental Technician MOS established 12 December 1947.

Dr. Mary Walker: Physician, MOH

Dr. Walker's unique life bridges the gap between military and civilian experiences. Both veterans and VA employees can share identify. She subtly gives strength to a necessary Jungian Archetypical Dimension via von Franz. Dr. Walker should have another statue made and placed in the foyer of VA Headquarters by *Dust Off*. Plaques of others should be placed in all VA Facilities.

COL GERALD FINK, USMC: POW KOREA, CAMP DENTIST

Col. Fink was my idol/mentor/patient. Col. was a Korea POW 3½ *Clicks* and voted Poyktong's Camp Dentist. For their Sky Pilot he carved the body of Jesus from scrub oak and Crown of Thorns made with scraps of radio wire akin to barbed wire. The Cross is cherry wood. It took almost 3 months to complete. His carving knife came from a boot's steel arch and chisel made out of irrigation pipe. He fashioned crowns and bridges using bone. Col. talked of such things when we were alone. When the Vietnam POW's returned and the press covering arrival, Col. shut me down and spent the rest of the day telling many other Dark Sides. I've seen. All is now clear. *My FIRST Lesson Learned Continues Stronger:*

It still exists: →

CDR MAURICE JOSES, MC, USN, USMC: POW PHILLIPINES, XO BILIBID

Maurice was my mother's cousin. By far older. She would on occasion lament how she missed him. Do not know why some eulogies also put USMC designation. Cousin's son, Elliott Joses, is a Naval Academy graduate and Marine Corps helicopter pilot.

LT Richard Guthrie, MC, USNR: CHILD POW, PHILIPPINES

Dr. Richard Guthrie's father was a Seventh Day Adventist hospital administrator in Japan before Americans were expelled. His father transferred to the Philippines. At age 11 Dr. Guthrie was first at John Hay and later reunited with family at Los Banos.

Steward Pueblo: North Korea Captive

One of the two non-rated Philippine Stewards of the Pueblo was stationed at MCRD San Diego at the same time Col. Fink and I were there. All Dental personnel were ordered to have no contact. His gold dental work was rifle-butt extracted.

FUTURE
MAKE A POSITIVE, ACTIVE FORWARD MOVEMENT NOW: *CYA*

Mandated Report Protocol involves Counseling first. Inclusive in my Appeals is such to *all* levels within Veterans Affairs, though not able to communicate directly. Let's move up. Please give me and my DAV Representative Mr. Hoy Evans a *Collegial* court date. If VA allows Appeals to perform recommendations in Judicial Activism subsiding bureaucratic meddling from *outside agencies*, will help write it up, abating much but not all. (See: Col. Wayne Rich). Do not want this extended. 12 years lost has been too destructive. I use the term *Homicide* Forensically correct. Non Deployed Tactical Reserves through *Linkage Analysis*, connecting Patterns, in part:

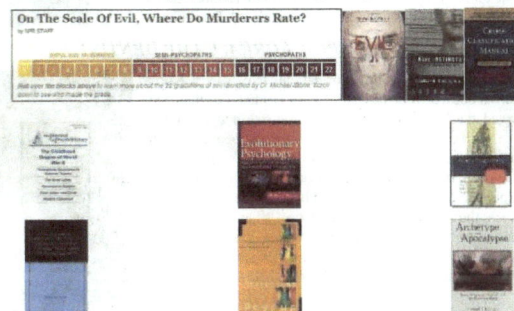

Every Death is an Apocalyptic Event

WE all are caught in solvable problems. VA patients could have been ours first. As VA patients we bridge the gap. Grand Strategy, Strategy, Tactics set. Select Personnel need more contact. Supply to VA. Deploy Logistics. *You Must Do Something.* Alter present course. Social Purpose requires cohesive group involvement. VA must lace up and *Arise*: however you decide to do so. Choose well *your* journey's path in →

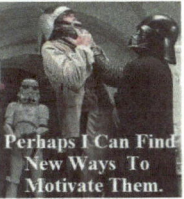

Essential Spirit

There is no sin in falling.
Sin is in not getting up and moving forward.
Arise with inner Spirit. Left foot first.
Never stop. Never quit. If tired, walk… Crawl.
Col. Gerald Fink, (*DC*), USMC

II: Definitions, Terms and Patterns of Behavior

CDR Richard L. Matteoli, DC, USN (ret.), FMF

May this addendum regarding VA *Forensic Cultural Anthropology* prove helpful to all, in their own particular way, who are involved in the quest for the expansion of knowledge.

 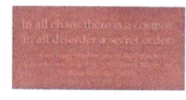
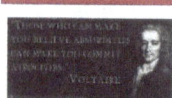 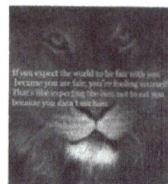

DEFINITIONS

Dissociation is the separation of the humanity of another individual to object status therefore a psychological lessening of the humanity of another that may lead to criminal behavior.

DISSOCIATE: **1.** To separate from association or union with another: DISCONNECT **2.** DISUNITE

DISSOCIATION: **1.** The act or process of dissociating: the state of being dissociated **b:** the separation of idea or activity from the mainstream of consciousness of consciousness or of behavior esp. as a mechanism of ego defense **2.** *Psychiatry* **a:** A psychological defense mechanism in which specific, anxiety producing thoughts, emotions, or physical separations are separated from the rest of the psyche **b:** the separation of a group of mental processes or ideas from the rest of the personality, so that they lead an independent existence,

DISSONANCE: **1.** Lack of agreement; *specif:* inconsistency between the beliefs one holds or one's actions and one's beliefs: DISCORD

DISSONANT: **1:** marked by dissonance: DISCORDANT **2:** INCONGRUOUS **3:** harmonically unresolved – **dissonatly** *adv*

> *Abuse involves every aspect of society and crosses all social ethnic, religious, and professional lines... Definition can range from a narrow focus, limited to intentional inflicted injury, to a broad scope, covering any act that adversely affects the development and potential... Included in the definition are neglect (acts of omission) and physical, psychological (acts of commission). INTENT [of the perpetrator] is NOT considered in reporting abuse.*[1]

RES IPSA LOQUITUR: **The thing speaks for itself.**

From *Law Dictionary* by Steven H. Gifis[2]

REAL EVIDENCE: an object relevant to facts in issue at trial, 329 N.E. 2d 880, 885, and produced for inspection at trial rather than described by a witness. 259 S.E. 2d 5510, 533. Real evidence may include any object produced for inspection at trial, from a murder weapon to a tape recording of a telephone conversation or a photograph of where an event occurred to the exhibition of a physical injury. Real evidence is one type of **demonstrative evidence**. See, McCormack Evidence §§212-217 (2nd ed. 1975).

REALIZATION: the occurrence of an event or transaction deemed to be s sufficiently substantial change in the **taxpayer's** economic situation to warrant the imposition of an **income tax**. 348 U.S. 426. If the tax is imposed, the event gives rise to **recognition**. Thus, if a taxpayer buys an asset for $10 and sells it for $20, the sale constitutes a realization of the amount received. If the amount received in excess of the taxpayer's cost basis, it is considered **recognized**. GAIN OR LOSS REALIZED the difference between the amount realized on a **sale or exchange** of an asset and the taxpayer's **basis** in such asset.

REARGUMENT: the oral presentation of additional arguments to a court after it has already heard argument, for the purpose of demonstrating that "there is some decision or principle of law which would have a controlling effect and which been overlooked, or that there has been a misapprehension of facts." 18 N.Y.S. 2d 107, 110. Re-argument usually occurs prior to the court rendering a decision in a matter and may be distinguished from a **rehearing** which also presents some new or overlooked principle of law or fact but which usually occurs after the court has rendered its decision.

REASONABLE BELIEF: in criminal law, similar to the **probable cause** standard is that it is a subjective standard used to validate a **warrantless search and seizure** or **arrest** and that considers whether an officer acted on personal knowledge of facts and circumstances which are reasonably trustworthy, and that would justify a person of average caution to believe that a crime has been or is being committed

REASONABLE CARE: "that degree of **care** which under the circumstances would ordinarily be exercised or might be reasonably expected from an ordinary prudent person." 268 So. 2d 290, 292. The exercise or absence of reasonable care.., a jury question, is often depositive of tort cases involving injury to others.

REASONABLE DOUBT: refers to the degree of certainty required for a juror to legally find a criminal **defendant** guilty… The term "reasonable doubt" does not signify a mere skeptical condition of the mind. Nor does it require proof be so clear as to eliminate any possible error as to eliminate any possibility of error since under such a rule no criminal prosecution would prevail. It means simply that the proof must be so conclusive and complete that all reasonable doubts of the fact are removed from the mind of the ordinary person, see 25 F. 556, 558, or "would cause prudent men to hesitate before acting in matters of importance to themselves." 367 F. Supp. 91, 101.

REASONABLE MAN [PERSON]: a hypothetical who exercises "those qualities of attention, knowledge, intelligence and judgment which society requires of its members for the protection of their own interests of others." Restatement Torts 2d, §283(b): a test used to determine whether or not one person was **negligent** towards another. Negligence will exist upon a failure to do "something which a reasonable man, guided by those considerations which ordinarily regulate the conduct of human affairs, would do, or [the doing of] something which a reasonable and prudent person would not do." 43 S.W. 508, 509.

REASONABLE TIME: a subjective standard based on the facts and circumstances within a particular case, with applicability in a number of contexts..; to inspect goods prior to payment or acceptance, U.C.C. §2-513(1), 148 N.W. 2d 385, 389; to await performance by a party who repudiates a contract, U.C.C. §2-610(a);

2

TERMS

COGNITIVE DISSONANCE[3-6]
The mental stress or discomfort experienced by an individual who holds two or more contradictory beliefs, ideas, or values at the same time, or is confronted by new information that conflicts with existing beliefs, ideas, or values. *see*: Dismissive Cognition where psychopathy, individual and social, has no conflict present regarding results of their actions.

PASSIVE INITIATION[7-8]
The act of getting someone else to perform an act instead of doing the act themselves, *see*: Charles Manson. Sometimes the victim passively initiates simply by making a VA disability claim within the *Lifestyle Theory*. VA Passive Initiation may be exampled by:

1). *Administrators having those they supervise perform tasks of a criminal nature.*

2). A patient seeking Opiates and obtaining drugs from their physician as was the case of a problem address by the OIG and Congress with the over prescription of Opiates by the San Francisco Region.

3). *Refusing to necessary Liver Monitor the effects of tuberculosis medications during therapy*.

MEDICAL PATERNALISM 2.05[9]
One of the most common ethical issues raised by the principle of respect for autonomy is paternalism. The term refers to the practice of overriding or ignoring a person's preferences in order to benefit them or enhance their welfare. In essence, it consists in the judgment that beneficence takes priority over paternalism. Historically, the medical profession has endorsed paternalism. Today, while still common it is considered ethically suspect.

PATIENT PREFERENCE[10]
In all medical treatment, the preferences of the patient, based on the patient's own values and his or hers personal assessment of the benefits and burdens, are ethically relevant. In every clinical case, the questions must be raised: what are the patient's goals? What does the patient want? The systematic review of this topic requires further questions. Has the patient been provided sufficient information? Does the patient comprehend? Is the patient consenting voluntarily? Has the patient been coerced?

PATTERNS OF BEHAVIOR

MASLOW'S HIERARCHY OF NEEDS

Maslow, unlike most, studied motivation in normal and exemplary people as well as top students. Maslow discovered 5 elemental steps from basic survival to the apogee of life lived. The process is lineal where a step must be reasonably met before proceeding to the next. Regression occurs when an element at a lower becomes lost. Briefly they are: Physiological, Safety, Love and Belonging, Esteem; and lastly, Self-Actualization.[11-15]

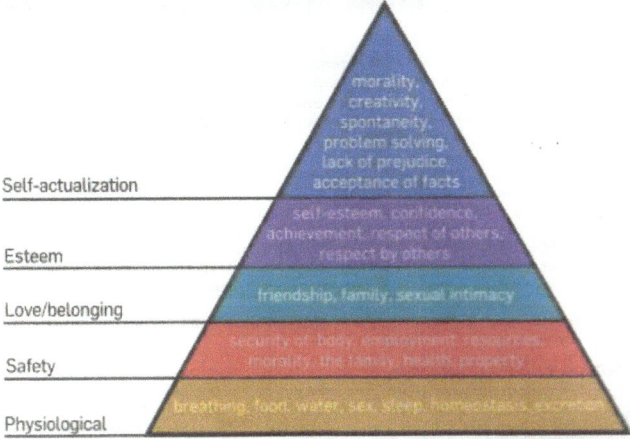

Many veterans seeking disability compensation exist within the 2 lower rung of Maslow's Hierarchy of Needs. Historic Patterns of Behavior of Veterans Affairs include grave instances of a criminal nature that exacerbate their tenuous position. It is as if they are kept imprisoned to the whims of those in power in Veterans Affairs in which they are: *in the care of*.[16]

Responsibility of those who have the veteran *in the care* of their employment does not reside alone with those giving treatment. Responsibility is as much if not more in certain areas and aspects of health care by those directing and driving policies and procedures whether official policy or unofficial policies which may be contradictory to Veterans Affairs.

PHYSIOLOGICAL
  Breathing, food,
  water, sex, sleep,
  homeostasis,
  excretion
                                 Hello   I am creation

SAFETY
  Security of: body,
  employment,
  resources,
  morality, family,
  health, property
                                 A job???   Home Sweet Hootch

LOVE and BELONGING
  Friendship,
  Family,
  sexual intimacy
                                 My Family begins   Work is nice

ESTEEM
  Self-esteem,
  confidence,
  achievement,
  respect of others,
  respect by others
                                 Narcissism Hazard   Malignant Narcissism

SELF-ACTUALIZATION
  Morality, creativity,
  spontaneity, problem
  solving, lack of prejudice,
  acceptance of facts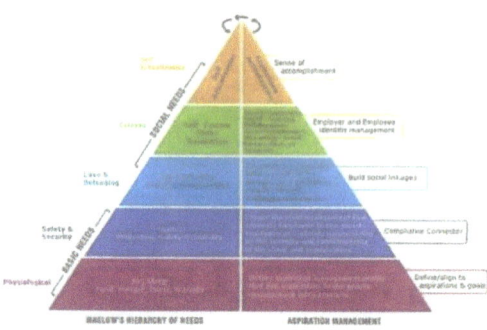
                                 Humility   I am as God is

5

TRANSACTIONAL ANALYSIS

Eric Berne's Transactional Analysis (TA) discusses the types of *communication*. Communication segments psychology into three 'negotiating' *ego* elements, *Parent*, *Adult* and *Child*, abbreviated as PAC. Parent and Child communication is mediated through the Adult. Berne's categories are similar but not identical with Freud's psychology as: Parent/ego, Adult/superego and Child/id.[17-19]

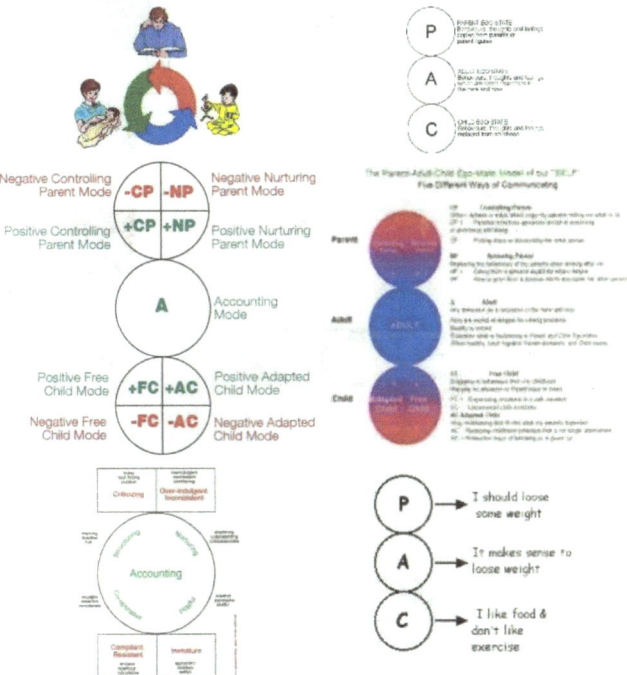

Communication displays a format with Transactional Analysis. From Berne's *Games People Play*:[20]

TRANSACTION
The unit of social intercourse is called a *transaction*. If two or more people encounter each other in social aggregation, sooner or later one of them will speak, or give some other indication of acknowledging the presence of others. This is called 'transactional stimulus.' Another person will say or do something which in some way related to this stimulus, and that is called the 'transactional response.' Simple transactional analysis is concerned with diagnosing which ego state implemented the transactional stimulus, and which one executed the response. The simplest *transactions* are those in which both stimulus and response arise from the Adults of the parties concerned. The agent, estimating the data before him that a scalpel is now the instrument of choice, holds out his hand. The respondent appraises this gesture correctly, estimates the forces and distances involved, and places the handle of the scalpel exactly where the surgeon expects it. Next in simplicity are Child-Parent transactions. The fevered child asks for a glass of water, and the nurturing mother brings it. Both these transactions are 'complimentary;' that is, the response is appropriate and expected and follows the natural order of healthy human relationships.[21]

PROCEDURE
A *procedure* is a series of simple complementary Adult transactions directed toward the manipulation of reality... *Procedures* are based on data processing and probability estimates concerning the 'material' of reality, and reach their highest development in professional techniques... Two variables are used in evaluating *procedures*: A *procedure* is said to be 'efficient' when the agent makes the best possible use of the data and experience available to him, regardless of any deficiencies that may exist in his knowledge. If the Parent or the Child interferes with the Adult's data processing, the *procedure* becomes 'contaminated' and will be less efficient. The 'effectiveness' of a *procedure* is judged by the actual results. The efficiency is a psychological criterion and effectiveness is a material one.[22]

RITUAL
A *ritual* is a stereotyped series of simple complementary transactions programmed by external social forces. An informal *ritual*, such as social leave-taking, may be subject to considerable local variations in details, although the basic form remains the same. A formal *ritual*, such as a Roman Catholic mass, offers much less option... Many formal *rituals* started off as heavily contaminated though fairly efficient procedures, but as time passed and circumstances changed, they lost all procedural validity while still retaining their usefulness as acts of faith. Transactionally, they represent guilt-relieving or reward-seeking compliances with traditional Parental demands. They offer a safe, reassuring (apotropaic), and are often an enjoyable method of structuring time.[23]

PASTIMES
This may be defined as a series of semi-ritualistic, simple, complementary transactions arranged around a single field of material, whose primary object is to structure of time. The beginning and the end of the interval are typically signaled by procedures or rituals. The transactions are adaptively programmed so that each party will obtain the maximum gains or advantages during the interval. The better his adaptation, the more he will get out of it.[24]

GAME
> A *Game* is an ongoing series of complementary ulterior transactions progressing to a well-defined, predictable outcome. Descriptively it is a recurring set of transactions, often repetitious, superficially plausible, with a snare, or "gimmick." Games are clearly differentiated from procedures, rituals and pastimes by two chief characteristics: (1) their ulterior quality and (2) the payoff. Procedures may be successful, rituals effective, and pastimes profitable, but all of them are by definition candid, and ending may be sensational, but it is not dramatic. Every *Game*, on the other hand, is basically dishonest, and the outcome has a dramatic, as distinct from exciting, quality.[25]

CODEPENDENT THINKING

Codependent Thinking involves 9 modes of thinking that are involved in and lead to dysfunctional relationships:[26]

BLACK AND WHITE THINKING
> is any negative thing that happens gets turned into a Sweeping Generality.[27]

NEGATIVE FOCUS
> is always thinking a glass is half empty, not half full. The other extreme is focusing on the positive to deny feelings.[28]

MAGICAL THINKING
> is often in ritual to replace reality and a way of creating a self-fulfilling prophesy.[29]

STARRING IN A SOAP OPERA
> involves blowing tings out of proportion. Users become the King or Queen of Tragedy. They are *trauma dramas*. Intensity of dramatic scenes in conflict are common themes. Individual overindulgence predominates.[30]

SELF-DISCOUNT
> includes the inability to receive, or to admit to our own positive qualities.[31]

EMOTIONAL REASONING
> is from feeling by believing that we feel is who we are, without separating the inner Child's feelings and Adult feeling in the present.[32]

SHOULDS,
> *musts*, and *have tos*, come from authority figures. Adults do not have *shoulds* – Adults have choices.[33]

SELF-LABELING
> identifies our perceived shortcomings and imperfections by not accepting one's humanity.[34]

PERSONALIZING THE BLAME
> is blaming oneself as personally and totally responsible for happenstance, and how someone else feels. Conversely, it is blaming other people, or fate, to one's attitudes and behavior that may have contributed to a problem.[35]

RETURNING TO KEVIN FITZMAURICE
TRIPARTATE NATURE OF THE EGO: Part I

Fitz Maurice explains that the ego has only five actions with many variations:[36-38]

1. Seek death and destruction
2. Cover death and destruction with darkness
3. Cover death and destruction with names of good
4. Cover calling evil good (#3) with darkness
5. Cover death and destruction with victim role

Maurice then explains these as ego responses to threat or disturbance from:

1. Pain, hurt, shame, loss of face, humiliation
2. Fear of ego pain
3. Anger, fighting
4. Anxiety, avoidance, fear, escapism, flight

FREUD: THANATOS

Importance of Fitz Maurice is that the focus of ego functions is within Freud's *Thanatos* commonly known as the Death Wish as opposed to the Pleasure Principle which resides in our survival instinct through Eros and may apply to deep seated id manifestations within Veterans Affairs. Eros and Thanatos appear to represent the Light-life aspect of existence whose opposite side of this concept's coin is Dark-death.[39-41] Aspects of the definition include:

Psychiatry

1. A desire for self-destruction, often accompanied by feelings of depression, hopelessness and self-reproach.
2. The desire, often unconscious, for the death of another person, such as a parent, toward whom one has unconscious hostility.
3. A suicidal urge thought to drive certain people to put themselves consistently dangerous situations.
4. *Psychology (in Freudian psychology)* the desire for self-annihilation. See also *Thanatos*.
5. *(Classical Myth & Legend)* the Greek personification of death: son of Nyx, goddess of night and Erebos, god of darkness and his twin brother Hypnos, sleep. Siblings included: Geras – old age; Oizys – suffering; Moros – doom; Apate – deception; Momus – blame; Eris – strife; Nemesis – retribution and even Charon the ferryman who transported newly deceased across the rivers Styx and Acheron into Hades. Roman counterpart: Mors.

Thantalos, by using WWI as an example, allowed Freud to explain man's desire for murder and destruction including the fact that the death-drive is stronger than the life-drive.

Repetition Compulsion is closely bound to Thanatos and the need to repeat traumatic events in order to deal with and give a sense of control over them. Repetition Compulsion is an aspect of *Maslow's Self-actualization Hierarchy of Needs*. The sense of self-actualization, thus living at the top of the ladder, requires psychic reinforcement and successful Patterns of Behavior will be repeated. The drive for psychic fulfillment in Criminology is termed a *ritual*.[43-54]

ETHOS

Eddy Bernays' wrote *Propaganda* in 1928 and used by Joseph Goebbels in charge of Nazi propaganda. Bernays considered the general population – *The Herd* – and inferior. He observed:[55]

*The conscious and intelligent manipulation of the organized habits and opinions of the masses is an important element in democratic society. Those who manipulate this unseen mechanism of society constitute an invisible government which is the true ruling power of our country. We are governed, our minds are molded, our tastes are formed, our ideas suggested, lately by men we have never heard of. This is a logical result of the way in which our democratic society is organized... In almost every act of our daily lives, whether in the sphere of politics or business, in our social conduct or our **ethical thinking**, we are dominated by the relatively small number of persons... It is they which pull the wires which control the public mind.*

Dissociation requires a change in ethical behavior with rationalizing away wrongs. This may occur under stress.[56-58] Robert Solomon wrote *A Short Introduction to Philosophy* and related with last paragraph relates Carol Gillian's retort to Lawrence Kholberg:[59]

Inductive logic: does not guarantee the truth of the conclusion, but only makes it more reasonable for us to believe the conclusion compared to other possible conclusions
Deductive logic: guarantees the truth of the conclusion, if the premises are true

Psychological egoism: All acts are basically selfish
Ethical egoism: You ought to act selfish
Psychological altruism: Some of our acts are basically altruistic
Ethical altruism: You ought to act for the good of others

Rationalism: Knowledge is based on reason
Necessary Truth: A statement that true because of reason
Empiricism: Knowledge is based on experience
Empirical Truth: A statement is true because of the facts

Moral Relativism: There are no universal and essential moral values, that morality is 'relative' to particular societies or peoples.
Ethical Relativism: the thesis that whatever a culture or a society holds to be right is therefore right, or, at least right for them.
Moral absolutism: the thesis that there are universal and essential moral values. If some society or people do not accept these values, then they are not moral.

Rather than thinking of ethics in terms of impersonal, abstract, moral principles of right and wrong, claimed Gillian, women tend to think of ethics in terms of moral personal responsibility. While men understood a moral dilemma posed by the experimenter as a problem having a right and wrong answer, women understood such a dilemma as the result of an interpersonal conflict in need of a resolution, not a right-versus-wrong answer. Gillian hypothesized that in addition to the moral reasoning grounded in abstract principles of right and wrong described by Kant and Kohlberg, there is also a more "feminine" but equally valid type of moral reasoning that is grounded in maintaining the stability of interpersonal relationships.

Moral evil is a product of our actions

CULTURAL PROGRESSION

Social Psychology concentrates on any and all aspects of human behavior. It involves our relationships to other persons, groups, social institutions, and to society as a whole. This includes clinical-social behavior.[60] Summaries:

ASSOCIATION

Psychosocial growth and development implies association with other individuals. Much of a person's mental content comes from others including beliefs, standards, values and ideals. Customs are powerful. And institutions of power, control, and authority with their laws in government, religion, social mores and ceremony are somewhat static because *prestige* lies in *precedent*, which is to say a type of *antiquity*. Thus a person's experiences are connected in subordination to the group's leading principles. But, leading principles evolve over time through *suggestive* interaction and are not static, uniform, or final. Stasis, uniformity, and finality attach themselves to closed scientific systems like mathematics but the open system of the human mind does not restrict pursuits like language, literature or religion.[61]

ACTS

Social acts or behavior, whether collective or individual, often have the purpose of influencing and controlling others. *Acts*, as surgery, that modify objects are *technical acts*. Acts that elicit pleasure or avoid pain are *hedonistic acts*. *Esthetic acts* are those that give meaning to an object (veteran). Besides the final outcome, that object becomes the *social token*. Tokens are used in all rituals by the Ritual Agent, whether the Ritual Agent is an individual or the culture itself. Tokens are often taken by criminals in similar manner to a sports trophy to be used to relive the successful experience.[62]

ACCULTURATION

A change in an original culture from contact with another culture or many cultures. This is different from *assimilation*, where different groups come together to form a new way of life. *Acculturation* deals with survival, resistance, modification, adaptation, and destruction of the old culture. *Diffusion* is adopting another culture's practice independent of population movement.[63]

CULTURAL APPROPRIATION

Occurs when a culture adopts an introduced behavior.[64]

CULTURAL IMPERIALISM

The phenomenon of an incoming group forcing new practices in their adopted culture.[65]

SOCIALIZATION

Socialization of new employee into the existing culture is *enculturation*. *Enculturation* is established through communal reinforcement by repeating the values and norms of the society to the new employee regardless of the lack of evidence to support society's, VA's, position. *Introjection* occurs when such behaviors become unconsciously accepted in the new employee's personality. *Introjection* is *internalization* of identification with parental figures, supervisors, and other aspects of the person's known world. Introjection is often accompanied with coping defense mechanisms and are forms of denial, self-deception, and deferral and are, as well, essential in *ritual*.[66]

GROUP DYNAMICS
Involves behavior to current happenings. This behavior differs according to the individual's response to the local group. To achieve a new agreement the barriers of prejudices, expectations, ideology, theology, and control must be overcome. This can give rise to *social constructionism* which creates a perceived reality. The new reality birthed in social constructionism is an invention of the culture that eventually appears obvious and as natural knowledge. This then establishes a *consensus reality* that is the reality the group or culture wishes to believe.[68-69]

PEER PRESSURE
Peer Pressure then imposes the group norm on individuals and requires people to conform. Peer Pressure works when *opinion leaders* prevail.[70]

GROUPTHINK
Is when people intentionally go along with what they think is the group's opinion. *Groupthink* leads to improper and non-logical decisions. It uses the need of people to belong with others. Symptoms of *groupthink* include:[71]
1. illusion with invulnerability from unity
2. unquestioned belief
3. group rationalization
4. stereotyping opponents
5. self-censorship
6. direct pressure to conform
7. self-appointed guardians

COMMUNAL BEHAVIOR
Community reinforces *collective behavior* by instilling *fear*. *Collective Hysteria*, at times, is imbedded to ignite social change as well as maintain social stasis.[72]

STRUCTURATION
Structuration is repeating leader positions with implied *special knowledge* who set rules for others to live by. These people are acting as the *social agent* in an effort to change people's behavior. This *agency* is also used by the social agent to *repress*.[73-74]

INSTITUTIONALIZATION
The overall successful result is *institutionalization*. Success expands (as perceived VA Oakland with VA Phoenix appear to have collaborated in criminal behavior, possibly as well the Radiologist in VA LA).[75] *Cultural Imperialism* is set.

SOCIAL NORM
Once a Social Norm is established it becomes easily enforceable. Violations of norms are punished., even if only through social shunning. Violators are thought to be eccentric and alternatives are not acknowledged.[76]

MORES
Mores are strongly held norms and customs and customs, similar to social norms, that increase the ability to isolate detractors from society.[77]

FOLKWAY
The endpoint is to establish and maintain a folkway that are strictly reinforced.[78]

MEME
A *meme*, introduced by Dawkins in *The Selfish Gene*, is the pathway of cultural practice and may be thought of as a *social gene*. It is an element of culture or system of behavior that may be considered to be passed from one individual to another by non-genetic means. A successful *meme* is a part of cultural tradition. It may be a tune, an idea or catch-phrase that remains in people's memories and capable of rapid evolution into society. As genes, *memes* are passed on through the *meme pool* being transmitted from brain to brain which, in a broad sense, can be called *learning* or *imitation*.[79]

PROGRESSION OF SOCIAL MOVEMENTS
Social Movements may be positive or negative according to a person's personal ethics. *Mobilization* toward a new social reality is generated when current social procedures are deemed improper and it is thought a new social order will provide an improved social experience. *Rebellion* and *changes* produced from mobilization create a new social tendency. The following 3 systems work in unison in the creation Social Movements:[80-82]
1. A *social situation* usually starts with an idealized purpose. Advocates of that ideal work together to create a new social system. Examples can include governments, economic systems or religions.
2. The *social act* puts the social purpose into effect.
3. *Social tendency* evolves from the perception of the social act as the proper way to behave. Then it becomes static behavior until a new social situation enters to correct any problems created by the original social situation, act or tendency.

SOCIAL ORDER
Social order refers to a set of interlocking social structures, social institutions and social practices that conserve, maintain and enforce group defined *normal* ways of behaving and relating that are considered essential control and order in the society. The *social order is forced* on the individual. *Social sublimation* occurs with conformity to and psychological acceptance of the *social ideal*. With cognizance a positive reaction occurs with acceptance of the social ideal and *social value* system are met. A negative occurs with unacceptance and will be met with a corresponding negative to *maintain stability*. *Social defense* occurs if the negative originates from outside the *social order*.[83]

SOCIAL OBJECT
The VA's *Social Object* is the veteran.[84-85]

OBJECT PERSON
An *object person* is someone who has been dehumanized due to an attribute or physical quality they possess. The object person will accept whatever happens if it does not conflict with their concept of the *social purpose*. If the person objects then psychological inner conflict occurs. The perpetrator, the *ritual agent or parental figure*, is likewise conflicted when the victim's doubt attempts the perpetrator's desired action. This inhibits the *original social act* and the perpetrator must then resort to making *claims* and *arguments* in support of his *social ideal* as a counter moral force to inhibit the *object person's* moral protestations. Or, the perpetrating *social force* may impose *repression*. Repression creates opposing social values that must eventually be resolved. *Moral standards* are part of social values that, when improper, are often held by *manipulative arguments* that restrict contradiction.[86]

REFLECTED SELF IMAGE
How does the victim, here the veteran, feel about himself or herself after being forced to submit to improper VA practices? The inner, internalized, *Reflected Self Image* of the veteran is altered due to the overwhelming power of the VA's *social forces*. The prevailing *social personality*, through a Social Agent's self-image, has essentially told him or her they must submit or be shunned as when Dr. Daniel in Ukiah told the staff, two of which I worked with at Indian Health before their VA employment, that I was not to be medically appointed. But if the person removes himself from the overpowering social process, if possible, and uses logical, objective thought, it will lead him to end the social subjugation. When this happens the social body in identity crisis must necessarily take steps to maintain itself hopefully with the correction of impropriety.[87-88]

DEPENDENCE
Dependence also means that other people are opportunities by others *imposing* their conceptual way of life, *imago vivendi*, onto others. That can be used personally and socially for one's selfish gratification and fulfillment. This leads to conflict when needs, wants desires and perception among individuals or groups differ. When successful, social movements overwhelm individual choice, free will and human rights.[89]

INTERDEPENDENCE
Interdependence entails personal and societal responsibilities. We subsist through the monetary *reward* our *occupations* provide. They are not simply jobs; they carry significant *responsibilities*. The question we must ask is whether the occupation's *service* or *contribution* to society is more beneficial, mischievous or harmful.[90]

ASSERTIONS – OFFICIAL POSITIONS
To be an acceptable member of a group a person needs to conform to certain codes of conduct termed *cohort codes*. For this the social organization adopts *official positions*. Official positions of impropriety are *justified* through manipulative *advise* and *decisions* from self and/or social *authority figures*.[91]

GROUP-FANTASY
Lloyd DeMause's *Foundations of Psychohistory* documents social abuse, often generational, by illustrating 3 causes: **1)**: the unified group; **2)**: the effect of the group's abuse on the individual; and, **3)**: the individual's subsequent responses back to the group. *Group-Fantasy*:[92-94]

A group-fantasy, then, is produced by a collection of social alters as an agreement by groups of people to pool their traumas into a delusional social construction. Social alters have 4 main characteristics:

1. separate neural memory modules that are repositories for traumatic events and accompany feelings frozen in time.

2. organized into dynamic structures containing a different set of goals, values and defenses than the main self that help prevent the traumas and resulting despair from overwhelming one's life.

3. split off by a senseless wall of denial, depersonalization, discontinuity of affect and disownership of responsibility that is maintained in collusion with others in society who have similar alters to deny; and

4. communicated, elaborated and acted out in group-fantasies embedded in political, religious and **social institutions***.*

GENOCIDAL "PURIFICATION"

Those responsible for Veterans Affairs (VA) in Oakland and VA Phoenix along with the outside possibility of at least VA Los Angeles and VA Salem, Oregon appear to have set an Organized Behavior requiring subordinates to conform. There is also the possibility that those responsible were prior initiated to their criminal activities. Pierre Bordieu wrote:[95]

> *Ultimately, when the strategies of ritualization are dominated by a special group, recognized as official experts, the definition of reality that they objectify works primarily to retain the status and authority of the experts themselves.*
>
> *Specific relations of domination and subordination are generated and orchestrated by the participants themselves simply by participating.*
>
> *It is this type of control that must be understood. These bodies of knowledge act simultaneously to secure a particular form of authority.*

Purification Rituals are concerned with Social Pollution and are formed through the use of *Collective Guilt*. Catherine Bell stated:[96]

> [Ritual, Bell quoting Steven Lukes] *helps define as authoritative certain ways of seeing society: it serves to specify what in society is of specific significance, it draws people's attention to certain forms of relationships and activities – and at the same time, therefore, it deflects their attention from other forms, since every way of seeing is also a way of not seeing.*
>
> [Bell] *Ultimately, the struggle between the individual psyche and society is never seen as simply out there in the social arena, but within each person as well. The formulation of ritual often to involve a distancing within actors of their private and social identities.*
>
> **The only real alternative to negotiated compliance is either total resistance or asocial self-inclusion.**

Carl Jung in *The Undiscovered Self* observed:[97]

> *In this broad band of unconsciousness, which is immune to conscious criticism and control, we stand defenseless, open to all kinds of influences and psychic inflections. As with all dangers, we can guard against the risk of psychic inflection only when we know what is attacking us, and how, where and when the attack will come. Since self-knowledge is a matter of getting to know the individual facts, theories help very little in this respect. For the more a theory lays claim to universal validity, the less capable it is of doing justice to the individual facts. Any theory based on experience is necessarily "statistical;" that is to say, it formulates an ideal average" which abolishes all exceptions at either end of the scale and replaces them by an abstract mean. This means is quite valid, though it need not necessarily occur in reality...*
>
> *The statistical method shows the facts in the light of the ideal average but does not give us a picture of their empirical reality. While reflecting an indisputable aspect of reality, it can falsify the actual truth in a most misleading way. This is particularly true of theories which are based on statistics. The distinctive thing about real facts, however, is their individuality. Not to put too fine a point on it, one could say that the real picture consists of nothing but exceptions to the rule, and that, in consequence, absolute reality has predominately the character of irregularity.*

15

Robert Lifton in his book *Nazi Doctors; Medical Killing and the Psychology of Genocide*, developed the concept of Doubling. This is different than Constructive Displacement that allows a surgeon the ability to cut into a patient to cure the patient as much as a parent cleaning a child's wound. Lifton stated:[98]

> *If you are curing a sickness "anything" is possible. The image of cure leads itself to the restorative myth of state violence and to the literal enactment of that myth.*
>
> *The key to understanding how Nazi doctors came to do the of Auschwitz is the psychological principle I call **doubling**: the division of the self into two functioning wholes, so that a part-self acts as the entire self. An Auschwitz doctor could, through doubling, not only kill and contribute to killing but organize silently, on behalf of that evil project, an entire self-structure (or self-process) encompassing virtually all aspects of his behavior.*
>
> *In doubling, one part of the self "disavows" another part. What is repudiated is not reality itself – the individual Nazi doctor was aware of what he was doing via the Auschwitz self – but the meaning of that reality. The Nazi doctor knew that he selected, but did not interpret selections as murder. One level disavowal, then, was the Auschwitz self's altering of the meaning of murder; and on the other, the repudiation by the original self of "anything" done by the Auschwitz self.*
>
> *Indeed, disavowal was the life blood of the Auschwitz self.*
>
> *Doubling can include elements considered characteristic of "Psychopathic" character impairment.*
>
> **Doubling may well be an important psychological mechanism for individuals living within any criminal substructure.**
>
> *Genocide is a response to collective fear of pollution and defilement.*
>
> *Purification tends to be associated with sacrificial victims, whether in primitive or contemporary religious or secular terms.*
>
> *It becomes an all-or-none matter, equally absolute in its claims to truth and in its rejection of alternate claims.*
>
> *The Nazis tapped mythic relationships between healing and killing that had ancient expression shamanism, religious purification, and human sacrifice, and evoked all three in ways that reveal more about their psychological motivations.*
>
> **One has to do this thing, see it through to the end, for the sake of utopian vision of national harmony, unity, wholeness.**

References

[1] Monteleone, James A., *Recognition of Child Abuse for the Mandated Reporter*, G. W. Medical Publishing, 1996, p. 1.

[2] Gifis, Steven H., *Law Dictionary*, Barron's Educational Series, 1984, pp. 386-388.

[3] Festinger, Leon, *A Theory of Cognitive Dissonance*, Stanford University Press, 1957.

[4] Festinger, Leon, (1962). "Cognitive Dissonance," *Scientific American*, 207, (4): 93-107.

[5] Aronson, E; Carlsmith, J.M., (1963). "Effect of the severity of threat on the devaluation of forbidden behavior," *Journal of Abnormal and Social Psychology*, 66 (6): 584-588.

[6] Aronson, E.; Mills, J., (1956). "The effect of severity of initiation on liking for a group," *Journal of Abnormal and Social Psychology*, 59: 177-181.

[7] Lee, Spike W. S.; Schwartz, Norbert, May (2010). "Washing Away Postdecisional Dissonance," *Science*, 328, (5979): 709.

[8] Anderson, James F., *Criminological Theories*, 2nd Edition, Jones and Bartlett, 2015, pp. 48-49.

[9] Johnson, Seigler, Winslade, *Clinical Ethics*, 3rd Edition, McGraw Hill, 1984, p. 39.

[10] Johnson, Seigler, Winslade, *Clinical Ethics*, 3rd Edition, McGraw Hill, 1984, p. 5.

[11] Maslow, Abraham, *Motivation and Personality*, Harper, 1954.

[12] Maslow, Abraham, *A Theory of Human Motivation*, Martino, 2013.

[13] Maslow, Abraham, *Maslow on Management*, Wiley, 1998.

[14] Maslow, Abraham, Maslow, Bertha, Geiger, Henry, *The Farther Reaches of Human Behavior*, Penguin, 1993.

[15] Maslow, Abraham, *Toward a Psychology of Being*, Sublime Books, 2014.

[16] Kay, Susan, "*The Constitutional Dimensions of an Inmate's Right to Health Care*, National Commission on Correctional Health Care by the Corrections and Sentencing Committee, Criminal Justice Section of the American Bar Association, 1991.

[17] Berne, Eric, *Games People Play*, Harper, 1967.

[18] Harris, Thomas, *I'm OK – You're OK*, Avon Books, 1973.

[19] Herzberg, F.; Mausner, Bernard; Snyderman, Barbara, *The Motivation to Work*, Transaction Publishers, 1998.

[20] Berne, Eric, *Games People Play*, Harper, 1967, pp. 29, 35-36, 36-37, 41 and 48.

[21] Wang, X. T.; Simons, F.; Bredart, S. (2002). "Social cues and verbal framing in risky choice," *Journal of Behavioral Decision Making*, 14 (1): 1-15.

[22] Scott, Michael L., *Programming Language Pragmatics*, Morgan Kaufmann, 2009.

[23] Bell, Catherine, *Ritual Theory, Ritual Practice*, Oxford University Press, 1992.

[24] Tudor, Keith, *Transactional Analysis Approaches to Brief Therapy: What do you say between saying hello and goodbye?*, Sage, 2002.

[25] Harmon-Jones, E. (2004). "Contributions From Research On Anger And Cognitive Dissonance To Understanding The Motivational Functions Of Asymmetrical Frontal Brain Activity," *Biological Psychology*, 51-76.

[26] Burney, Robert, *Codependence / The Dance of Wounded Souls*, Joy to You & Me Enterprises, 1995.

[27] Guess, Andrew, *Taking Sides: Changing Views in Life-Span Development*, McGraw-Hill/Dushkin, 2012.

[28] McGregor, Douglas, *The Human Side of Enterprise*, McGraw-Hill, 2006.

[29] Estes, Clarissa Pinkola, *Women Who Run With the Wolves: Myths and Stories of the Wild Woman Archetype*, Ballantine, 1995.

[30] Alexander, A.; Ayerman, R.; Giesen, B.; Smelser, N.; Sztompka, P., *Cultural Trauma and Collective Identity*, University of California Press, 2004.

[31] Holstein, James A.; Gubrium, Jaber F., *The Self We Live By: Narrative Identity in a Postmodern World*, Oxford University Press, 1999.

[32] Ciarrochi, Joseph, *Emotional Intelligence in Everyday Life*, Psychology Press, 2001.

[33] Andrews, Matt, *The Limits of Institutional Reform in Development: Changing Rules for Realistic Solutions*, Cambridge University Press, 2013.

[34] Brown, Jonathon, *The Self*, Psychology Press, 2014.

[35] Goleman, Daniel, *Social Intelligence: The New Science of Human Relationships*, Bantam, 2007.

[36] FitzMaurice, Kevin, *Ego Playground*, FitzMaurice Publishers, 2014.

[37] FitzMaurice, Kevin, *Breath*, FitzMaurice Publishers, 2010.

[38] FitzMaurice, Kevin, *The Secret of Maturity*, FitzMaurice Publishers, 2012.

[39] Freud, Sigmund, *Beyond the Pleasure Principle*, Norton, 1990.

[40] Freud, Sigmund, *The Ego and the Id*, Norton, 1990.

[42] Freud, Sigmund, *The Psychopathology of Everyday Life*, Norton, 1990.

[43] Freud, Sigmund, *Group Psychology and the Analysis of the Ego*, Norton, 1990.

[44] Freud, Sigmund, *Civilizations and Its Discontents*, Norton, 2010.

[45] Jung, Emma, *Animus and Anima*, Spring Publications, 1985.

[46] Douglas, John; Burgess, Ann; Burgess, Allen; Ressler, Robert, *Crime Classification Manual: A Standard System for Investigating and Classifying Violent Crime*, Jossey-Bass, 1997.

[47] Banning, Peter, *Breaking the Cycle: A Fresh Look*, Xlibris, 2000.

[48] Michaud, Steven; Hazelwood, Roy, *The Evil That Men Do*, St. Martin's, pp. 81-98.

[49] Keppel, Robert with Birnes, William, *Signature Killers: Interpreting the Calling Cards of the Serial Murderer*, Pocket, 1997.

[50] Kelleher M.; Kelleher, C., *Murder Most Rare: The Female Serial Killer*, Dell, 1998.

[51] Jensen, Jaclyn M.; Opland, Richard A.; Ryan, Ann Marie. (2010). "Psychological Contracts and Counterproductive Work Behaviors: Employee Responses to Transactional and Relational Breach," *Journal of Business Psychology*, 25: 555-568.

[52] Bass, Bernard M.; Avolio, Bruce J.; Atwater, Leanne. (1996). "The Transformational Leadership of Men and Women," *Applied Psychology: An International Review*, Vol. 45, Issue 1, 5-34.

[53] Maher, Karen J., "Gender-Related Stereotypes of Transformational and Transactional Leadership." *Sex Roles*, August 1997, Volume 37, Issue 3-4, pp. 209-225.

[54] Rauste-Von Wright, Maijalissa; Frankenhaeuser, Marianne. (1989). "Female's Emotionality as Reflected in the Excretion of Dopamine Metabolite HVA During Mental Stress," *Psychological Report*, Volume 64, Issue 3, pp. 856-858.

[55] Bernays, Eddie, *Propaganda*, ig Publishing, 1928, pp. 9-10.

[56] Zhong, C. B.; Liljenquist, K.; (2006). "Washing away our sins: Threatened morality and physical cleansing," *Science*, 313, (5792): 1451-1452.

[57] Gachter, S.; Nosenzo, D; Sefton M., (2010) "Peer effects in pro-social behavior: Social norms or social preferences," *Series Paper 2010-2023*, (retrieved), University of Nottingham.

[58] Mills, J., (1968). "Changes in moral attitudes following temptation." *Journal of Personality*, 26 (4): 517-531.

[59] Solomon, Robert, *A Short Introduction to Philosophy*, p. 326

[60] Cooper, J.; Axsom, D.' *Integration of clinical and social psychology*, Oxford University Press, (2007).

[61] Keisler, C. A.; Pallak, M. S. (1976). "Arousal properties of dissonance manipulations," *Psychological Bulletin*, 83 (6): 1014-1025.

[62] Beckman, J.; Kuhl, "Altering information to gain action control: Functional aspects of human information to gain action control: Functional aspects of human information processing in decision making," *Journal of Research in Personality*, 18 (1984), pp. 224-237.

[63] Petty, R. E.; Brinol, P.; DeMasrree, K. G. (2007). "The Meta-Cognitive Model (MCM) of attitudes: Implications for attitude measurement, change, and strength," *Social Cognition*, 25 (5): 657-686.

[64] Van Overall, F.; Jordens, K. (2002). "An adaptive connectionist model of cognitive dissonance," *Personality and Social Psychology Review*, 6 (3): 204-231.

[65] Monroe, B. M.; Read, S. J.. (2008). "A general connectionist model for attitude structure and change: The ACS (Attitudes as Constraint Satisfaction) Model," *Psychological Review*, 115 (3): 773-759.

[66] Hart, W.; Albarracin, D.; Eagly, A. H.; Brechan, I.; Lindberg, M. J.; Merriull, L. (2009). "Feeling validated versus being correct: a meta-analysis of selective exposure to information," *Psychological Bulletin*, 135 (4).

[67] Engestrom, Yrjo; Miettinen, Reijo,; Punamaki, Raija-Leena, *Perspectives on Activity Theory: Learning in Doing*, Cambridge University Press, 1999.

[68] Ryan, Carey S.; Bogart, Laura M. (Oct. 1997). "Development of new group members' in in-group and out-group stereotypes: Changes in perceived variability and ethnocentrism," *Journal of Personality and Social Psychology*, 73 (4): 719-732.

[69] Pinto, I. R.; Marques, J. M.; Abrams, D. (2010). "Membership status and subjective group dynamics: Who triggers the black sheep effect?," *Journal of Personality and Social Psychology*, 99 (1): 107-119.

[70] FitzMaurice, Kevin, *Ego Playground*, FitzMaurice Publishers, 2014.

[71] Wilcox, Clifton, *Groupthink*, Xlibris, 2010.

[72] Gully, S. M.; Devine, D. J.; Whitney, D. J. (1995). "A Meta-analysis of Cohesion and Performance: Effects of Level of Analysis and Task Interdependence," *Small Group Research*, 26 (4): 497.

[73] Bell, Catherine, *Teaching Ritual*, Oxford University Press, 2007.

[74] Bell, Catherine, *Ritual: Perspectives and Dimensions*, Oxford University Press, 2009.

[75] Deaux, D.; Reid, A.; Mizrahi, K.; Ethier, K. A. (1995). "Parameters of social identity," *Journal of Personality and Social Psychology*, 68 (2): 280.

[76] Sherif, M., *The psychology of social norms*, Harper, 1936.

[77] Turner, J. C. (1975). "Social comparison and social identity: Some prospects for intergroup behavior," *European Journal of Social Psychology*, 5:1.

[78] Sumner, William Graham, *Folkways*, Library of Alexandria, 2012.

[79] Dawkins, Richard, *The Selfish Gene*, 2nd Edition, Oxford University Press, 1990.

[80] Chen, M. K.; Risen, J. L. (2010). "How choice affects and reflects preferences: Revisiting the free-choice paradigm," *Journal of Personality and Social Psychology*, 99 (4): 573-594.

[81] Sharot, T.; Velasquez, C. M.; Dolan, R. J. (2010). "Do decisions shape preference? Evidence from blind choice," *Psychological Science*, 21 (9): 1231-1235.

[82] Izuma, K.; Matsumoto, M.; Murayama, K.; Samejima, K.; Sadato, N.; Matsumoto, K. (2010). "Neural correlates of cognitive dissonance and choice-induced preference change," *Proceedings of the National Academy of Sciences, USA*, 107 (51): 22014-22019.

[83] Wenger, Etienne, *Communities of Practice: Learning, Meaning and Identity*, Cambridge University Press, 2000.

[84] Qin, J.; Kimel, S.; Kitayama, S.; Wang. X.; Han, S. (2010). "How choice modifies preference: Neural correlates of choice justification," *Neuroimage*, 55 (1): 240-246.

[85] Jarcho, Johanna M.; Berkman, Elliot T.; Lieberman, Matthew D., "The neural basis of rationalization: cognitive dissonance reduction during decision-making," *Social Cognitive Affective Neuroscience*, Sept. 2011; 6(4): 460-467.

[86] Fointiat, V. (2004). " 'I know what I have to do, but...' When hypocrisy leads to behavioral changes," *Social Behavior and Personality*, 32: 741-746.

[87] Fein, Steven; Spencer, Steven J., "Prejudice as Self-Image Maintenance: Affirming the Self Through Derogating Others," *Journal of Personality and Social Psychology*, 1997, Vol. 73, No. 1, 31-44.

[88] Bem, D. J. (1967). "Self-perception: An alternative interpretation of cognitive dissonance phenomena," *Psychological Review*, 74 (3): 183-200.

[89] Festinger, L.; Carlsmith, J.M., (1959). "Cognitive consequences of forced compliance," *Journal of Abnormal and Social Psychology*, 58 (2): 203-210.

[90] Bem, D. J. (1965). "An experimental analysis of self-persuasion," *Journal of Experimental Social Psychology*, 1 (3): 199-218.

[91] FitzMaurice, Kevin, *Garbage Rules*, FitzMaurice Publishers, 1st Edition, 2012.

[92] deMause, Lloyd, *The Social Alter*, Presented at the 18th Annual Convention of the International Psychohistory Association, 07 June 1995, New York City, New York.

[93] deMause, Lloyd, *Foundations of Psychohistory*, Other Press, 2002.

[94] deMause, Lloyd, *The Emotional Life of Nations*, Creative Roots, 1982.

[95] Bordieu, Pierre, *Outline of a Theory of Practice*, Cambridge University Press, 1977, pp. 184, 40-41, 207 and 98-108.

[96] Bell, Catherine, *Ritual Theory, Ritual Practice*, Oxford University Press, 1992, pp. 173, 216, and 215. Lukes, Steven, (1975). "Political Ritual and Social Integration," *Journal of Sociological Association*, Vol. 9, No. 2, 289-350.

[97] Jung, Carl, *The Undiscovered Self*, Mentor, 1958, pp. 16-17.

[98] Lifton, Robert, *Nazi Doctors; Medical Killing and the Psychology of Genocide*, Basic Books, 1986, pp. 418, 422-423, 488, 482, 484, 470-471, 482-483 and 199.

I: Definitions, Terms and Patterns of Behavior

CDR Richard L. Matteoli, DC, USN (ret.), FMF

May this prove helpful to all, in their own particular way, who are involved in the quest for the expansion of knowledge.

  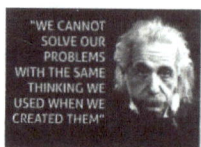

DEFINITIONS

ALTRUISTIC ETHOS: a postured form of argument or discussion to enhance a belief or position as it relates to humanity in general

BABELIAN IMPERATIVE: 1. The act of deceiving through use of a euphemism. 2. The use of language in deception through obfuscation

BERNAYS EFFECT: the improper and successful manipulation of an individual, group or the general public for power, control, and authority or financial gain see: Eddie Bernays: Logical Fallacies (Power of Words), Persuasion Analysis, Propaganda Techniques, Public Relations

DISMISSIVE COGNITION: putting aside Cognitive Dissonance, or absence thereof, to accommodate a behavior and/or acting on a belief system due to individual, interpersonal and/or societal lack of empathy

COLLECTIVE GUILT: guilt of a collective group whether valid or not

COLLECTIVE MUNCHAUSEN IN SOCIAL AGENCY: The agency relationship between the person with a primary agency, usu. a parent or caregiver, and another person who accepts secondary agency, usu. a doctor or shaman, that creates an act of abuse.

COLLECTIVE MUNCHAUSEN SYNDROME FOR PROFIT: occurs with group activity, with the motive for profit, that involves the abuse of a child.

DELIBERATE DIFFERENCE: setting apart an individual or identifiable group, either expressly or by mute sanction, for different laws, equality, equity, actions, or inactions toward

DOMESTICATED VIOLENCE: socialized and/or acculturated use of violence in Transference of Aggression personally and/or interpersonally often detrimental to self and others in ritualistic behavior

IATROGENIC PATHOPHYSIOLOGY: pathophysiology caused by agency usu. as a result from a physician, or another, acting as a health care provider

LEGAL TRIANGLE: is the basis for settling disputes involving Justice-Injustice; Administrative Morality-Congressional Ethics in which right-wrong tests legal-illegal where the Equity Center is *value*.

```
                    JUSTICE (JUDGE) INJUSTICE
                              /\
              ADMINISTRATIVE /  \ CONGRESSIONAL
                MORALITY    /    \   ETHICS
                           / VALUE \
                          /_____\

      RIGHT (PLAINTIFF) WRONG < = > LEGAL (DEFENDANT) ILLEGAL
```

MALIGNANT HERO SYNDROME: a person or group of persons who falsely and often maliciously create a crisis then miraculously rush in to solve the problem they created in a self-glorification

MUNCHAUSEN SYNDROME FOR PROFIT: is the fabrication of disease or exacerbation of an existing medical condition by a person, often with a specialized agent as an attorney or special interest group, to gain sympathy from others and/or society for financial gain. see: Quid Pro Quo

MUNCHAUSEN SYNDROME IN COLLECTIVE TRANSMISSION (MSICT): is a delusional transmission of a condition or simulation of disease taken to clinical significance whether to a person or another person or group of persons. It is the transference of alleged identity to a personal relationship, family, community, society, or culture. It operates by deliberate transmission from one generation to subsequent generations of unresolved conflicts, dependencies, and aggressions onto a substitute body object of heirs.

MUNCHAUSEN SYNDROME IN SOCIAL TRANSFERENCE (MSIST): is the identity transference of the self into a social group that practices forms of Munchausen behavior

SOCIALIZED STALKING: organized improper social behavior directed toward an individual or group

TRANSFERRED COLLECTIVE GUILT: 1. The transference of guilt onto an identifiable group from the actions of another or others. 2. Applied collective guilt by substitution through denial, deception, and deferral

TRANSFERRED GUILT: 1. transference of guilt onto an identifiable group from the actions of another or others. 2. applied collective guilt by substitution through denial, deception, and deferral

TRANSFERRED REPRESENTATION: a transference of identity of an object, a person or objectified body part imparting new meaning that may create an altered meaning or focus of attention whether consciously or unconsciously directed

TRANSGENERATIONAL MUNCHAUSEN SYNDROME (TMS): is generational abuse in family and social groups and a step toward acculturation

TERMS

ANXIETIES[1]

Neurotic Anxiety: has to do with separation from an object perceived as a whole and separate from you, problems with sexual identity, loss of one's body

Psychotic Anxiety: has to do with questions of survival or annihilation, the question of separation from something of which you are a part (or which is a part of you), and problems with identity

DIFFUSION OF RESPONSIBILITY (Bystander Effect; Attribution)[2]

A sociopsychological phenomenon whereby a person is less likely to take responsibility for action or inaction when others are present. Considered a form of attribution, the individual assumes others are either responsible for taking action or have already done so. The phenomenon tends to occur in groups of people above a certain critical size and when responsibility is not explicitly assigned. It rarely occurs when the person is alone and diffusion increases with groups of three or more.

FEAR CONDITIONING (Fear by Osmosis; see: Parable of the 5 Monkeys)[3-4]

Fear Conditioning is a behavioral paradigm in which organisms learn to predict aversive events. It is a form of learning in which averse stimulus (e.g. electrical shock) is associated with a particular neutral context (e.g. a room) or neutral stimulus (e.g. a tone), resulting in the expression of fear responses to the originally neutral stimulus or context. This can be done with pairing the neutral stimulus with an adverse stimulus (e.g. shock, loud noise, or unpleasant odor). Eventually, the neutral stimulus alone can elicit the state of fear. In the vocabulary of classical conditioning, the neutral stimulus or context is the "conditional stimulus" (CS), the aversive stimulus is the "unconditional stimulus" (US), and the fear is the "conditional response" (CR).

MODUS OPERENDI and SIGNATURE[5]

Modus Operandi - MO – is learned behavior. It's what the perpetrator does to commit the crime. It is dynamic – that is, it can change.

Signature, a term I [Douglas] coined to distinguish it from MO, is what the perpetrator has to do to fulfill himself. It is static; it does not change

TRANSFERENCE OF AGGRESSION

TRANSFERENCE: The deliberate displacement of one's unresolved conflicts, dependencies, and aggressions onto a substitute object

PATTERNS OF BEHAVIOR

MOTIVATIONAL CYCLE OF BETRAYAL
(Signature's Desire)

Cycle of Abuse

CYCLE OF POWER AND CONTROL
(Wheel of Violence)

A DEVELOPMENTAL PATHWAY OF SOCIAL PATHOLOGY

CULTURE BOUND SYNDROME
 A local pattern of aberrant behavior with troubling experiences. They do not become accepted social behaviors and considered a type of sickness in that society. Such behavior may be from *schadenfreude*, (German: schaden=damage; freunde=joy) a feeling of enjoyment that comes from seeing or hearing about others troubles. Socially and as well to the self, *schadenfreude* may extend to Culture Specific Syndromes.

CULTURE SPECIFIC SYNDROME
 A form of disturbed specific to a cultural system. Culture Specific Syndromes are considered normal behavior in that society. They may spread to other cultures from contact through Cultural Imperialism.

SHARED PSYCHOTIC DISORDER (Folie Imposee to Folie a Deux to Folie a Plusieurs)
 A delusion imposed on a person from a close relationship with another who already has a Psychotic Disorder with prominent delusions. The delusion in the second person is similar to the delusion of the person who already has a delusion and termed *Induced Delusional Disorder* (Folie Imposee).

 Shared Psychotic Disorder may develop in families (Folie en Famille). Family closeness may exist in group including social groups in work relationships. Extreme socialization creates Folie a Plusieurs).

 Left untreated Shared Psychotic Disorder becomes chronic and pervasive. Sometimes Major Sadism develops.

TRIPARTITE NATURE AND STRUCTURE OF EGO
Kevin Fitzmaurice

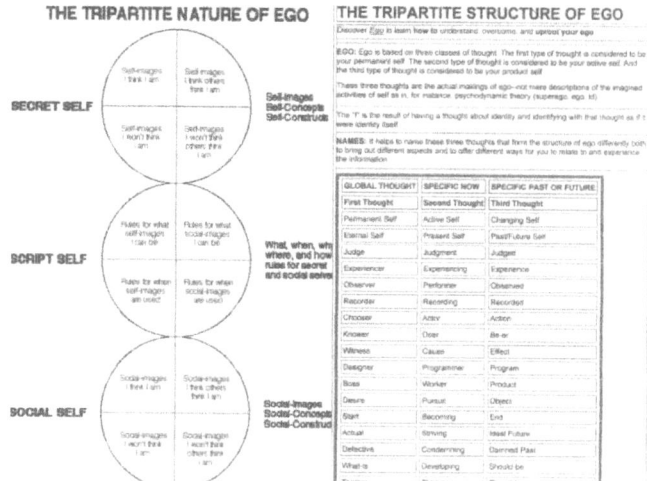

EDINGER'S SELF DEIFICATION FROM THE EGO-SELF RELATIONSHIP[6]
CREATING A HOSPITAL-RELIGIOUS SUBCULTURE: MENDELSHON:[7]

The hospital is the church
Doctors are the priests
Nurses are the nuns
Medications are the sacraments
X-rays and surgery are the rituals
Questioning or disobedience equates to heresy

All this within the schizophrenic condition Lifton termed Doubling in *The Nazi Doctors: Medical Killing and the Psychology of Genocide*, Basic Books, 1986 where he stated the thing they thought they were doing was as "constructive work in a slaughterhouse." See: pp. 210 and 418, 420-424 and 488.

ABUSER-ABUSED CYCLE OF EMOTIONS

Abuser-Abused Cycles include total internal individual emotions, actions and reactions in as well as existing in a cultural system where an abuser-abused cycle of behavior exists.

Repetition Compulsion – Generational Abuse

<u>Perpetrator</u> →   →   →   <u>Victim</u>

Distress arises from Betrayal   *Disfranchisement* from loss of privilege for immunity

Torment is increased with recurrent distress   *Self-esteem* is lowered

Anger evolves in a feeling of displeasure of one's condition   *Guilt* is the mantle taken regarding the Self

Hate is a result created   *Shame* is guilt's response in relation to others

Hostility becomes activated   *Ignominy* is the perceived Self; branded, disgraced, debased

Aggression follows from frustration   *Disgrace* becomes the place of existence

Violence onto another is perpetrated   *Humiliation* is the living existence

Rage is uncontrolled violence   *Envy* of others formulates

Wrath is a violent fit of rage   *Resentment* of others is envy solidified

Abuse is enacted to completion   *Desperation* is the attempt to reconcile Self existence

Justification is hypothesized to formality   *Hopelessness* in despair is reality of things unchangeable

<u>Victim</u> ←   ←   ←   <u>Perpetrator</u>

References

[1] Little, Margaret, *Transference Neurosis & Transference Psychosis*, Jason Aronson, 1993, pp. 167-168.

[2] Darley, JM & Latane, B. (1968). "Bystander intervention in emergencies: diffusion of responsibility," *Journal of Personality and Social Psychology*, 8, 377-383.

[3] LeDoux, Joseph, *The Emotional Brain: The Mysterious Underpinnings of Emotional Life*, Simon & Schuster, 1996.

[4] Maren, Stephen, (2001). "Neurobiology of Pavlovian fear conditioning," *Annal Review of Neuroscience*, 24: 897-931.

[5] Douglas, John with Olshaker, Mark, *Mind Hunter: Inside the FBI's Elite Serial Crime Unit*, Pocket Books, 1995, p. 252.

[6] Edinger, Edward, *Ego and Archetype: Individuation and the Religious Function of the Psyche*, Shambala, 1992, p. 3.

[7] Mendelshon, Robert, *Confessions of a Medical Heretic*. McGraw-Hill, 1990, pp. 58-59.

Tricare NOT Obamacare

It is easier to punish the compliant
Open Tricare to the public with civilian options

http://www.military.com/benefits/tricare

NOT

Just insurance
Existing government health insurance plan
System secure
Options available
Based on industry standards
No politics

INSURANCE

Tricare is the existing government based insurance policy for members of the United States military.

Meets Requirements of Health Care Reform Law

Privacy Policy
Fraud and Abuse within and to Insurance Laws
Within the No Fear Act

http://www.tricare.mil/

SECURITY

Security, both personal and insurance plan, is set to governmental and industry standards.

TMA Privacy and Civil Liberties Office
http://www.tricare.mil/tma/privacy/

Regulatory Requirements & Additional Resources
http://www.tricare.mil/tma/privacy/hipaa-legislation.aspx

OPTIONS

Multiple policy options include Gynecology and can add emergency dental for children.

Tricare Options Explained at length with reference sites
http://www.military.com/benefits/tricare/your-tricare-benefits-explained.html

NO POLITICS

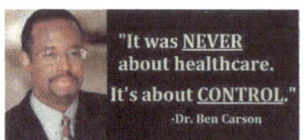

http://carsonscholars.org/dr-ben-carson/general-information

http://baltimore.cbslocal.com/2013/10/11/dr-ben-carson-making-waves-again-obamacare-worst-thing-since-slavery/

AGENCY CONFLICT

Tricare is under the Department of Defense, Defense Health Agency, strictly as a beneficial insurance program. Obamacare is under the Department of Health which sounds reasonable but structurally sets a Pretorian Guard under the Presidency that is directly loyal to the President and not the American people. It allows his Pretorian Guard type agency to actively work at his direction when the President declares a National Emergency. Funding for armed conflict belongs to Congress.

Such matters are now under the control of each State's Governor who uses his State National Guard. Local health care facilities with civilian health care professionals are present nationally. For Federal matters the United States Public Health Department which services Indian Health, Federal Prisons and the United States Coast Guard may be activated. Otherwise, during times of armed conflict, war, the United States Coast Guard is transferred to the Department of Defense.

Under more specifics, ultimate authority rests under each State's County Sheriff. Other avenues of establishing control might appear with the military purge and actions against County Sheriff authority. Matters that cross state lines are under the direction of the Federal Bureau of Investigation. There is no existing manpower deficiency for false hysteric concerns to set forth another federal power structure to control with Section 5210: ESTABLISHING A READY RESERVE CORPS.

Defense Health Agency
http://www.tricare.mil/tma/

Section 5210. ESTABLISHING A READY RESERVE CORPS, pp. 5-7
http://www.examiner.com/article/does-obamacare-establish-a-ready-reserve-police-force-part-2

3

CRONYISM

Existing Exemptions to Obamacare appear to be bases on Political Cronyism more likely than not through inappropriate Lobbying practices to at times possibly being linked to Campaign Contributions. The list of other factors that apply is extensive, in part: No Bid Contract to altering Pirated Software to run the program.

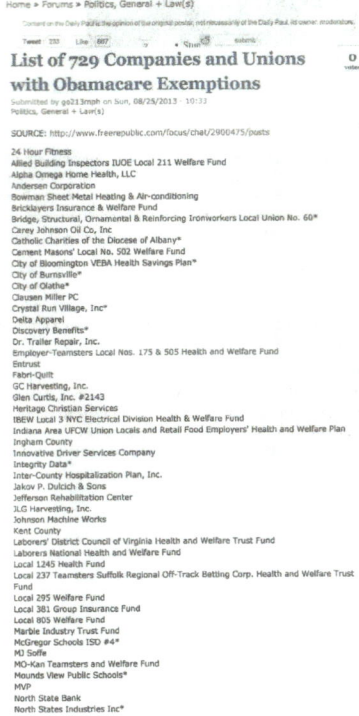

List of 729 Companies and Unions with Obamacare Exemptions

SOURCE: http://www.freerepublic.com/focus/chat/2980475/posts

24 Hour Fitness
Allied Building Inspectors IUOE Local 211 Welfare Fund
Alpha Omega Home Health, LLC
Andersen Corporation
Bowman Sheet Metal Heating & Air-conditioning
Bricklayers Insurance & Welfare Fund
Bridge, Structural, Ornamental & Reinforcing Ironworkers Local Union No. 60*
Carey Johnson Oil Co, Inc
Catholic Charities of the Diocese of Albany*
Cement Masons' Local No. 502 Welfare Fund
City of Bloomington VEBA Health Savings Plan*
City of Burnsville*
City of Olathe*
Clausen Miller PC
Crystal Run Village, Inc*
Delta Apparel
Discovery Benefits*
Dr. Trailer Repair, Inc.
Employer-Teamsters Local Nos. 175 & 505 Health and Welfare Fund
Entrust
Fabri-Quilt
GC Harvesting, Inc.
Glen Curtis, Inc. #2143
Heritage Christian Services
IBEW Local 3 NYC Electrical Division Health & Welfare Fund
Indiana Area UFCW Union Locals and Retail Food Employers' Health and Welfare Plan
Ingham County
Innovative Driver Services Company
Integrity Data*
Inter-County Hospitalization Plan, Inc.
Jakov P. Dulcich & Sons
Jefferson Rehabilitation Center
JLG Harvesting, Inc.
Johnson Machine Works
Kent County
Laborers' District Council of Virginia Health and Welfare Trust Fund
Laborers National Health and Welfare Fund
Local 1245 Health Fund
Local 237 Teamsters Suffolk Regional Off-Track Betting Corp. Health and Welfare Trust Fund
Local 295 Welfare Fund
Local 381 Group Insurance Fund
Local 805 Welfare Fund
Marble Industry Trust Fund
McGregor Schools ISD #4*
MD Soffe
MO-Kan Teamsters and Welfare Fund
Mounds View Public Schools*
MVP
North State Bank
North States Industries Inc*

11 pages of Exemptions
http://www.dailypaul.com/296870/list-of-729-companies-and-unions-with-obamacare-exemptions

MICROCHIP

The main concern about Congressional opposition to Obamacare appears to be the Medical Devise provision. It is also a very serious concern among many religious Christians that is a matter for discernment. If used solely for medical concerns it may be much better than a Medical Bracelet. As any technology it may be used for the good or once established altered for nefarious purposes.

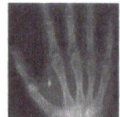

X-ray RFID Microchip: Courtesy Google Images

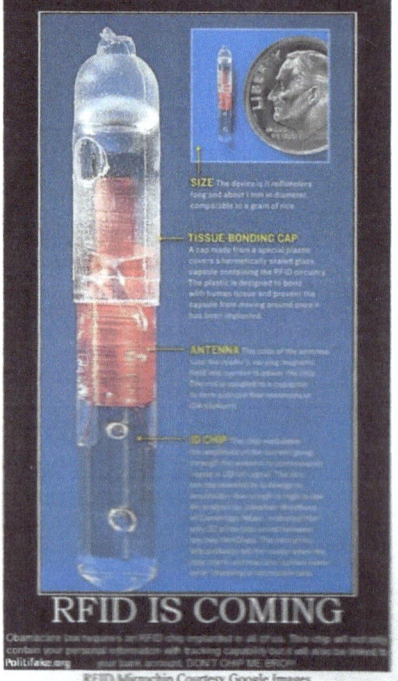

RFID Microchip.Courtesy Google Images

Lethal Dose can be incorporated.
Saudi made but patent denied.
Still exists.
http://www.youtube.com/watch?v=qCVVUuvXOoc

There are two types of RFID microchips.
1) Active RFID signal can extend 100 meters.
2) Passive RFID signal can extend 3 meters.
Both are accessible by WiFi that allows signals to be sent outside as well as into the medical setting including the Internet and many other systems in use today.

RFID Microchip: Cisco
http://www.cisco.com/en/US/docs/solutions/Enterprise/Mobility/wifich6.html

Stealth Medicine

Once government systems are established whether local, national or international monitoring is a necessity. One example is the STERILIZATION VACCINE used by the United Nation's World Health Organization, UNICEF, funded mostly by the United States with private benefactors.

Specific batches with their own Lot Code are used, to sterilize women. The active ingredient does not disallow fertilization but rather for her entire life she will never be able to carry a fetus to full term. The Philippine Supreme Court made it illegal to use in their country after they realized 7 million their females. It has also become an Israeli necessity for Ethiopian Jews to migrate into their country.

http://www.whale.to/b/bill_gates1.html

http://www.lifesitenews.com/news/archive//ldn/2004/mar/04031101

'Immuno-Sterilization' In Humans, A 2009 Vaccination Odyssey

By A. True Ott, PhD, ND
http://educate-yourself.org/cn/ottimmunosterilization25sep09.shtml
September 25, 2009

Immuno-Sterilization: In Humans, A 2009 Vaccination Odyssey, by Dr. A. True Ott (Sep 28, 2009)

source:
http://labvirus.wordpress.com/2009/09/26/a-true-ott-phd-nd-%E2%80%9Cimmunosterilization%E2%80%9D-in-humans-a-2009-vaccination-oddysey

According to the Los Angeles Sunday Times newspaper dated May 24, 2009, a meeting of some of the world's richest billionaires took place in Manhattan on **May 5, 2009**. (See addendum #1 below). These "elite" reached a uniform consensus during this meeting that OVERPOPULATION is the single greatest threat facing Planet Earth.

http://www.infowars.com/rockefeller-foundation-and-who-continue-collaboration-on-sterilizing-vaccines-implantables/

Rockefeller Foundation and WHO Continue Collaboration on Sterilizing Vaccines, Implantables

Jurriaan Maessen
Infowars.com
September 6, 2010

"The idea of harnessing the immune response to control fertility was first proposed in the 1950's. However, only recently has our comprehension of the immune system progressed to the level where the idea may finally be put into practice."

The Scientist Creative Quaterly, August 2003

As the World Health Organizations admits in its 2001 technical report Research on the Development of Methods of Fertility Regulation, research into both "injectable immunocontraceptives" and implantable ones has been long in the making, coordinated and developed in collaboration between the Rockefeller Foundation and the World Health Organization:

http://lifesitenews.com/news/archive/ldn/2004/mar/04031101

SUMMARY

Altruism in Obamacare is appropriate. Its precept is basic universal health care for the American public. Its modus is to make an insurance plan available for all to access.

The problem with Obamacare is its developed structure. Its grasp is too far reaching, lost in political governmental bureaucracy making it nonfunctional. From this structure non-medical loopholes have been created that are and may lead to further inappropriate behavior.

Cost - Empiricism vs. Culturalism
http://www.youtube.com/watch?v=IsVqOe07cdY

7

The hubris of politics and bureaucracy with regard to Obamacare is acting as a malignant narcissist to those under their care. Narcissists develop structures of destruction and impose that destruction upon those subservient to them. Those who said the bill should be passed and read later more likely than not knew what was being proposed. This is a type of Munchausen By Proxy taken to the social; thus, Munchausen Syndrome in Collective Transmission. The perpetrators are acting with threats to those under their care. And the threats are being carried out. Such is a Malignant Hero Syndrome.

If those making Obamacare were not exempt from prosecution they may be held liable for many of their actions including, in part, Child Endangerment, Financial Elderly Abuse to Civil Conspiracy. Prosecution would be under the Federal Tort Claims Act. Their criminal Approach is the Con.

Tricare with a civilian options is the proper alternative. Tricare is so successful that those in the military being forced to drop Tricare will be paying triple their current fees. With Universal Health the savings realized from reducing State programs could be used to help the Obamacare Tricare System.

Obama to Force Military Families Away From Tricare ...By Tripling Their Fees.

admin | On 29, Jun 2012

President Barack Obama has said on multiple occasions that he stands by the troops, and lauds their selflessness in fighting the Iraq war and the conflicts in Afghanistan. During a time when our bravest in uniform have been in a state of war for more than a decade, one would think that our fearless leaders should reward their efforts by making life a bit easier at home.

Instead, Obama simply insists on tripling their fees on the military health insurance program called Tricare.

What is the administration's reasoning on this? Well, they actually admit that Obama would rather the troops partake in 'alternatives' that were established in the Affordable Care Act (otherwise known as Obamacare). In a report from the FreeBeacon.com, Bill Gertz states:

> *Administration officials told Congress that one goal of the increased fees is to force military retirees to reduce their involvement in Tricare and eventually opt out of the program in favor of alternatives established by the 2010 Patient Protection and Affordable Care Act, aka Obamacare."*

This is quite a telling move by the Obama administration, due to the transparency in a letter written to Congress, as the FreeBeacon.com further reports:

> *The Administration is disappointed that the Congress did not incorporate the requested TRICARE fee initiatives into either the appropriation or authorization legislation," the White House wrote in an official policy statement expressing opposition to the bill, which the House approved in May."*

So, what are these "fee initiatives"? The Bill Gertz goes on to say,

https://www.ijreview.com/2012/06/9466-mugging-soldiers/

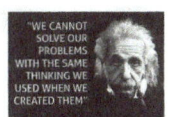

Einstein images Courtesy Facebook

Tricare NOT Obamacare

An open Mandated Report to the United States of America's Social Body.

8

Listen Here: Patriot Broadcast From the Trenches

Get together in our chat room: The Pub

Or you can mail donations to Henry Shivley at P.O. Box 964, Chiloquin, OR 97624

ICD 9: International Medical Coding and "Legal" Execution Brought Under Obamacare

Posted on November 22, 2013 by Paraclete

Uncle Sam Guillotine   Freedom Outpost – by Lorri Anderson

A faithful reader sent me a code and asked me to investigate how it ties into the larger scale of things. The specific code sent to me will make any American's hair stand up on the back of their neck. The code is ICD 9 E 978. After reading this code I decided that it was my duty to investigate further and get to the bottom of why we have a medical code in the United States for "Legal Execution." Below are my results.

> *ICD 9 E 978 "Legal Execution*
> *All executions performed at the behest of the judiciary or ruling authority [whether permanent or temporary] as:*
>
> - *asphyxiation by gas*
> - *beheading, decapitation (by guillotine)*
> - *capital punishment*
> - *electrocution*
> - *hanging*
> - *poisoning*

- shooting
- other specified means
- INJURY UNDETERMINED WHETHER ACCIDENTALLY OR PURPOSELY
- INFLICTED

According to reports, more than 68,105 new medical codes are being added due to the Obamacare monstrosity. Doctors all across the nation have been complaining due to the overwhelming burden it places upon them. Just the time consumption alone, making sure these codes are accurate, will inevitably take time away from the doctor/patient relationship creating a barrier of paperwork while destroying the personal experience with your doctor. While these doctors are correct to state it will be even more of a burden, they are not correct to state this has come out of Obamacare itself. Let me explain.

These codes were not created by Obamacare, however Obamacare is trying to implement every American citizen under international codes to link us to the "international" system. These codes were actually created by the WHO (World Health Organization). The WHO is a specialized agency of the United Nations.

First, it is important to know what the meanings of the codes are to grasp a better understanding of the importance and depth of this "internal takeover" that has been going on for many years right under our noses. The first ICD (International Classification of Diseases) was created in 1893.

- WHO took control of clinical modifications in 1948.
- 1955 the WHO modified the ICD to track mortality rates.
- 1977 the 9th revision was published aka "ICD 9 Medical Codes" that are being used today within our medical system.
- 1988 Congress passed "Medicare Catastrophic Coverage Act" requiring the use of ICD 9 codes on all claims.
- 1996 Mandated codes to be of highest possible specificity.

As of October 1, 2014 the ICD 9 coding will no longer be used. ICD 10 "mandated" medical coding will add 68,105 codes. The ICD-10-PCS (Procedure Code System) has an additional 86,000 codes totaling approximately 155,000 new medical codes for medical professionals. I can see why this would be overwhelming, and I am sure this will be a burden on doctors. One does have to wonder why doctors have not spoken out against this international coding system in the first place. This "international" United Nations based code is used to track people in all countries that have signed on with the WHO plan. Their "coding" and "data" collections have been implemented all around the globe with a few exceptions. So why are American doctors being required to use international medical coding? Why haven't doctors pointed out these are international codes? Why did congress sell out the American people in 1988 by passing the "Medicare Catastrophic Coverage Act" going along with and forcing "Sovereign United States Citizens" under "International rules, regulations, and coding"?

According to Wikipedia

The World Health Organization (WHO) is a specialized agency of the United Nations (UN) that is concerned with international public health. It was established on 7 April 1948, with its headquarters in Geneva, Switzerland. WHO is a member of the United Nations Development Group. Its predecessor, the Health Organization, was an agency of the League of Nations.

The use of the word "world", rather than "international", emphasized the truly global nature of what the organization was seeking to achieve. The constitution of the World Health Organization had been signed by all 61 countries of the United Nations by 22 July 1946. It thus became the first specialized agency of the United Nations to which every member subscribed. Its constitution formally came into force on the first World Health Day on 7 April 1948, when it was ratified by the 26th member state. The first meeting of the World Health Assembly finished on 24 July 1948, having secured a budget of US$5 million (then GBP£1,250,000) for the 1949 year.

Andrija Stampar was the Assembly's first president, and G. Brock Chisholm was appointed Director-General of WHO, having served as Executive Secretary during the planning stages. Its first priorities were to control the spread of malaria, tuberculosis and sexually transmitted infections, and to improve maternal and child health, nutrition and environmental hygiene. Its first legislative act was concerning the compilation of accurate statistics on the spread and morbidity of disease. The logo of the World Health Organization features the Rod of Aesculapius as a symbol for healing.

The WHO and the World Bank constitute the core team responsible for administering the International Health Partnership (IHP+). The IHP+ is a group of partner governments, development agencies, civil society and others committed to improving the health of citizens in developing countries. Partners work together to put international principles for aid effectiveness and development cooperation into practice in the health sector.

In addition, the WHO has also promoted road safety. Each year, the organization marks World Health Day focusing on a specific health promotion topic, timed to match the anniversary of WHO's founding. Recent themes have been drug resistance (2011) and aging (2012). As part of the United Nations, the World Health Organization supports work towards the Millennium Development Goals. Of the eight Millennium Development Goals, three – reducing child mortality by two-thirds, to reduce maternal deaths by three-quarters, and to halt and begin to reduce the spread of HIV/AIDS – relate directly to WHO's scope; the other five inter-relate and have an impact on world health.

The organization develops and promotes the use of evidence-based tools, norms and standards to support member states to inform health policy options. It oversees the implementation of the International Health Regulations, and publishes a series of medical classifications; of these, three are overreaching "reference classifications": the International Statistical Classification of Diseases (ICD), the International Classification of Functioning, Disability and Health (ICF) and the International Classification of Health Interventions (ICHI). Other international policy frameworks produced by WHO include the International Code of Marketing of Breast-milk Substitutes (adopted in 1981), Framework Convention on Tobacco Control (adopted in 2003) and the Global Code of Practice on the International Recruitment of Health Personnel (adopted in 2010).

The WHO regularly publishes a World Health Report, its leading publication, including an expert assessment of a specific global health topic. Other publications of WHO include the Bulletin of the World Health Organization, the Eastern Mediterranean Health Journal (overseen by EMRO), the Human Resources for Health (published in collaboration with BioMed Central), and the Pan American Journal of Public Health (overseen by PAHO/AMRO).

As of 2013, the WHO has 194 member states: all Member States of the United Nations except Liechtenstein, as well as the Cook Islands and Niue. (A state becomes a full member of WHO by ratifying the treaty known as the Constitution of the World Health Organization.)

As of 2013, it also had two associate members, Puerto Rico and Tokelau. Several other entities have been granted observer status. Palestine is an observer as a "national liberation movement" recognized by the League of Arab States under United Nations Resolution 3118. The Holy See also attends as an observer, as does the Order of Malta. In 2010, Taiwan was invited under the name of "Chinese Taipei".

WHO Member States appoint delegations to the World Health Assembly, WHO's supreme decision-making body. All UN Member States are eligible for WHO membership, and, according to the WHO web site, "other countries may be admitted as members when their application has been approved by a simple majority vote of the World Health Assembly". In addition, the UN observer organizations International Committee of the Red Cross and International Federation of Red Cross and Red Crescent Societies have entered into "official relations" with WHO and are invited as observers. In the World Health Assembly they are seated along the Financing and partnerships.

The WHO is financed by contributions from member states and outside donors. As of 2012, the largest annual assessed contributions from member states came from the United States ($110 million), Japan ($58 million), Germany ($37 million), United Kingdom ($31 million) and France ($31 million). The combined 2012–2013 budget has proposed a total expenditure of $3,959 million, of which $944 million (24%) will come from assessed contributions. This represented a significant fall in outlay compared to the previous 2009–2010 budget, adjusting to take account of previous under spends. Assessed contributions were kept the same. Voluntary contributions will account for $3,015 million (76%), of which $800 million is regarded as highly or moderately flexible funding, with the remainder tied to particular programs or objectives.

In recent years, the WHO's work has involved increasing collaboration with external bodies. As of 2002, a total of 473 NGOs had some form of partnership with WHO. There were 189 partnerships with international non-governmental organization (NGO) in formal "official relations" – the rest being considered informal in character. Partners include the Bill and Melinda Gates Foundation and the Rockefeller Foundation.

WHO and Bill

As you can see the WHO supports UN Agenda 21 through the "Millennium Development Goals" "Sustainable Development" agendas. President Obama, as senator, had a hand in attempting to increase U.S. political attention towards Millennium Development Goals, including The Borgen Project which worked with Senator Obama on "The Global Poverty Act"; a bill requiring the White House to develop a strategy for achieving the goals. The bill did not pass.

Even more disturbing, is finding out American citizens have been subject to the ICP Medial code for many years. Thus, giving the United Nations our private information through "coding." This is not only is an invasion of our privacy, but has been done in silence without our knowledge.

The Department of Homeland Security of Wisconsin "List of underlying causes of injury death Framework of E-code groupings

(ICD-9) 1989 – 1998" conveniently leaves out the definition of code ICD 9 E 978, but does reference it at the bottom of the list as: "1. Includes legal intervention (E970-E978) and operations of war (E990-E999)."

This certainly makes me wonder why DHS would omit ("hide") the code from the chart? Most people won't dig to find out what the "medical code" means unless they have a specific reason to do so. One thing is for sure, whether omitted by DHS or someone else, there is a good reason this code was left out of their document. They definitely didn't want most people to see what it means. DHS knows this code would create a stir with the American people if they found out there was a code for "Legal Execution," especially with a guillotine and beheading.

ICD9Data.com also gives a list for "legal intervention." Center for Disease Control "International Classification of Diseases, Tenth Revision (ICD-10)"

To read more about the "global" coding ICD 9 and 10 see below:
2013 ARHPC_ICD 9 CM

The questions that need to be asked and answered are:

1. Why has the United States been subjected to "International Medical Coding" without our knowledge?
2. Why are we allowing "coding" that goes against our principles and constitution?
3. Why do we have a code for "Legal Execution" which is illegal in America? With the exception of those given the death penalty after trial by jury.
4. When did the Department of Homeland Security find out about this coding? Why haven't they addressed this (since they are supposed to protect the people)?

1. Why is DHS sending any kind of "Medical Coding" to the states?
2. Why haven't the doctors spoken out to make Americans and Medicare recipients aware that their information has been given to an "International body"?
3. Why haven't they made people aware that the WHO is a specialized agency of the United Nations and directly linked to the "League of Nations under the guise of collecting data?
4. Why would we allow forced medical coding through congressional bills to come from an organization that supports UN Agenda 21, Millennium Development Goals, and supports

the eradication of "sprawl" (which is average people like you and I)?
5. Is law enforcement aware of this specific code? If so why haven't they brought this to the attention of the American people?

I, of course, do not know the answers to these questions, but I am deeply disturbed that we, the American People, have been kept in the dark on such an important issue. I was never asked permission for an international organization being able to access any of my information through "coding." I'll bet you were not asked either. It is bad enough the out of control IRS will have complete access to our health information. Now, to make matters even worse, we find out the WHO will have access to every American citizens health information through "medical coding," via Obamacare. When will enough be enough? When will the United States wake up and refuse to continue funding the United Nations and any organization that is affiliated with it?

One thing is for sure. This coding is directly related and tied to creating their "International One World Government." While the WHO pretends to be for helping people, they create codes for "Legal Execution" by beheading. The more you research, the more you realize that the WHO isn't all roses and sunshine. There is a much darker agenda at play. There is a direct connection between the "elitist" global banks and the WHO. The deeper you research, the more disturbing it gets. While American citizens have trusted our government to spend our money wisely, they have paid the WHO approximately $110 million dollars this year alone. Our government is inching us closer and closer to being controlled by a "One World Government" system and forcing us to pay for it. The repeal of Obamacare is important to our nation for many reasons, but pulling out of the United Nations and completely defunding them is imperative to our survival as a sovereign country and a free people.

Contact your representatives and demand that we defund and pull out of the United Nations now. Let them know about the "International Coding" system that is in place. I am sure many are not aware of this as they normally don't even read the bills before they pass them ref: Obamacare aka ACA. If they won't read their own bills why would we expect them to understand or know that the new medical coding is an expansion of a International Medical Code designed to track the world? This must be stopped. I am not and never have been a "global citizen"! I am an AMERICAN citizen!

I am Red, White, and Blue through and through, and will continue to fight for our country, exposing corruption and spreading truth as long as I live.

Read more: http://freedomoutpost.com/2013/11/icd-9-international-medical-coding-legal-execution/#ixzz2INfb0svV
Read more at http://freedomoutpost.com/2013/11/icd-9-international-medical-coding-legal-execution/#Yjp0lf34ADmgt6Pq.99

Share this:

Print   Email   Share 15   Share   Submit
G+1 1   Tweet   0

This entry was posted in News. Bookmark the permalink.
2556

One Response to ICD 9: International Medical Coding and "Legal" Execution Brought Under Obamacare

Slug Diamond says:
November 22, 2013 at 8:49 am

Wow, great article!

Reply

© 2010 - 2015 From the Trenches World Report

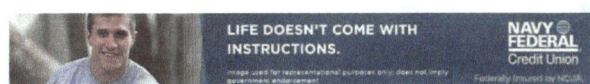

Commission to propose Tricare-like system for VA

Patricia Kime, Military Times 4:20 p.m. EDT June 7, 2016

A blue ribbon panel studying the future of Veterans Affairs health care is poised to recommend an overhaul to the system that would create a structure similar to the Pentagon's Tricare program, where veterans could choose to use either the VA for their care or see a network provider.

The goal, according to Commission on Care members, would be a more efficient version of the VA's current system, in which the department provides direct care to most veterans, and those who live more than 40 miles from a VA facility or who cannot get an appointment in a month offered private care.

(Photo: istockphoto)

Under the draft of the commission's final report, all veterans enrolled in VA care would choose a primary care provider at the VA or from a civilian network.

The plan would do away with the 30-day and 40-mile restrictions of the Veterans Choice program and create networks of physicians to care for former troops who prefer to see non-VA doctors.

The Commission on Care was created by Congress in 2014 under the legislation that established the Veterans Choice program. It is tasked with reviewing the VA health system and making recommendations on its future.

The panel's final report is due by the end of June but on Tuesday, commissioners met in Washington to revise a rough draft of the final.

MILITARYTIMES

Panel weighs closing all VA health care — vets' groups raise conflict of interest
(http://www.militarytimes.com/story/veterans/2016/04/01/panel-weighs-closing-all-va-health-care-vets-groups-raise-conflict-interest/82522000/)

That draft calls for creating a new structure, the VHA Care System, responsible for overseeing VHA facilities as well as preferred provider networks managed by contractors. An appointed board of directors would provide oversight to the entire Veterans Health Administration.

The draft calls for phasing in the new system, starting in areas where it is most needed. It also calls for giving VA the authority to close underperforming VA hospitals and clinics.

"Under this proposal, [VHA] becomes a care system, a more integrated model where every component of it is designed to deliver the best care to veterans," commission chairwoman Nancy Schlichting said.

The report also calls for giving some veterans who received other than honorable discharges access to VA health services. Under the draft, troops who have "substantial honorable service" before they got bad paper discharges would be considered for VA health care eligibility.

The proposal also considers allowing VA to establish pilot programs that would provide veterans and spouses the option to purchase health care at VA.

The estimated costs of these reform proposals were not available on Tuesday, but commissioners tossed out figures ranging from $100 billion to $1 trillion over 20 years.

Schlichting said many factors contribute to cost estimates, including demand, cost savings from closures and realignments and improving information technology systems.

But, she concurred, the reforms could be pricey.

MILITARYTIMES

Vets activists gearing up for 2016 fight
(http://www.militarytimes.com/story/military/benefits/veterans/2015/07/15/veterans-issues-2016-early/29922689/)

"I think we all agree if we increase choice, we increase costs," Schlichting said. "Given the level of reform we are recommending, [VA] is going to need resources."

The department last year began a reform process known as MyVA, which aims to fix issues ranging from health care quality and access problems to information technology problems and the benefits appeals backlog.

The 14-member commission has met 12 times since last September. Its work has been contentious, with veterans organizations, the White House and the VA speaking against any proposals to expand private care for veterans at the expense of VA medical centers and clinics.

The commission will send its final report to Congress this month. Whether lawmakers will act on it remains to be seen, however. The Senate and House are considering legislative proposals to change the Veterans Choice program, ranging from expanding it to all enrolled veterans to requiring most veterans use private care.

Follow @patriciakime

Patricia Kime covers military and veterans health care and medicine for Military Times. She can be reached at pkime@militarytimes.com (http://pkime@militarytimes.com)

Read or Share this story: http://militari.ly/1t6jLsi

Your **Money** Matters
Straight talk to help you make the most of your pay and benefits.

FirstCommand

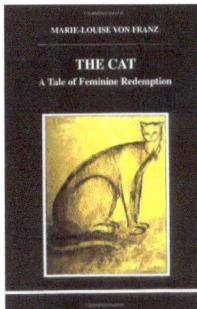  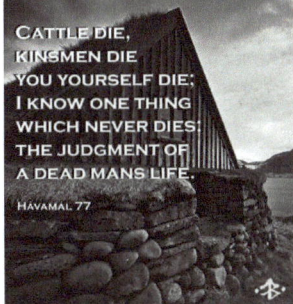

I am convinced that the hardest language to speak for some is the TRUTH.

I only say "bless you" twice.

If you sneeze a third time I assume it didn't take and that you're a demon who must be destroyed.

www.ingramcontent.com/pod-product-compliance
Lightning Source LLC
Chambersburg PA
CBHW041625220426
43663CB00001B/15